D0999061

Pruning
AN ILLUSTRATED GUIDE

First published in 2013 by Cool Springs Press, an imprint of the Quayside Publishing Group,
400 First Avenue North, Suite 400, Minneapolis, MN 55401

The information in this book is true and complete to the best of our knowledge. All
recommendations are made without any guarantee on the part of the author or Publisher,
who also disclaims any liability incurred in connection with the use of this data or
specific details.

Cool Springs Press titles are also available at discounts in bulk quantity for industrial or sales-
promotional use. For details write to Special Sales Manager at Cool Springs Press, 400 First Avenue North, Suite
400, Minneapolis, MN 55401 USA. To find out more about our books, visit us online at www.coolspringspress.com.

Library of Congress Cataloging-in-Publication Data

Lowe, Judy.
 Pruning : an illustrated guide : foolproof methods for shaping and trimming trees, shrubs, vines,
and more / Judy Lowe.
    p. cm.
 Includes bibliographical references and index.
 ISBN 978-1-59186-562-9 (softcover)
 1. Pruning. I. Title.

 SB125.L685 2014
 631.5'42--dc23
                              2013026162

Acquisitions Editor: Billie Brownell
Design Manager: Brad Springer
Design: Wendy Holdman
Layout: Kim Winscher
Front Cover Illustration: Melanie Powell
Illustrations: Pam Powell

Printed in China
10 9 8 7 6 5 4 3 2 1

Pruning

AN ILLUSTRATED GUIDE

FOOLPROOF METHODS
for Shaping and Trimming Trees,
Shrubs, Vines, and More

JUDY LOWE

COOL
SPRINGS
PRESS
Home and Garden Experts™

MINNEAPOLIS, MINNESOTA

Dedication & Acknowledgments

For Carlyle, who makes it all worthwhile.

Deepest thanks to everyone who has had such a big part in making this book the best it can be. It wouldn't have happened without the patience, organization, knowledge, and hard work of Billie Brownell, the best—and nicest—garden editor in the business. Her questions are always on target and make the final product more valuable to readers. Huge thanks to Pam Powell, whose drawings clearly illustrate the adage, "A picture is worth . . ."

My appreciation to Tracy Stanley, who finds all the problems and neatly picks them out, resulting in a more readable book. I'm deeply grateful to you all.

PRUNING
AN ILLUSTRATED GUIDE

The Benefits of Pruning

Y ou probably picked up this book because you have an overgrown shrub in your yard. Or you've moved to a house where all the shrubs were ignored by the previous occupant and now they've grown so large and daunting that you can't get from the front yard to the back by squeezing your way through the side yard. Should you hack those massively overgrown shrubs back by one-half or three-fourths and see if they'll grow back okay, or is there a way to prune them so they'll end up at a moderate size again and an attractive asset to your yard instead of a liability?

You already know that pruning can solve the problem of overgrown plants, making trees and vines, as well as shrubs, smaller, although you may not know the exact technique that best accomplishes that. But you may be surprised to learn that pruning also has many other benefits besides controlling a plant's size.

Why Prune?

You may prune to encourage shrubs, trees, roses, and vines to flower or fruit more abundantly and for the plants to grow more thickly, if needed, hiding undesirable views or providing more privacy. And correct pruning will guide plants' growth in the direction you need it to go, rather than where it's in the way. Pruning can prevent or correct damage to trees. (Have you ever seen a Bradford pear that split down the middle? Timely pruning might have prevented that.) Safety is another benefit of pruning. Avoid property damage by removing damaged limbs promptly, keeping tree branches from growing into power lines and reducing wind resistance in a top-heavy tree. (It's no fun after a wind storm, or even a brisk breeze, to be out in the yard picking up twigs and branches that have been knocked to the ground.) Quickly removing diseased or dying limbs from any plant helps protect the health of that plant—and also others in your yard, ensuring that the problem doesn't spread. People who live in cold climates will be pleased to learn that pruning trees in winter can make them more resistant to the damage caused by heavy snow loads.

Want your vines to yield more grapes or your apple trees to produce more and larger fruit? Your rosebushes to be covered with blooms? Prune them according to a few simple rules. That will also increase their longevity. The same is true for shrubs that have brightly colored stems or bark, which should be pruned yearly so the bush produces new growth that colors up well.

You can even put a monetary value on the benefits of regular pruning. Studies have shown that properly pruned and cared-for trees and shrubs in your yard increase your property value. They look healthy and neat, making your house seem much more like a desirable home.

Pruning can make it easier to use your yard for relaxation and play. When lower limbs of deciduous trees are removed (over a period of several years) so that they start about 10 feet or so from the ground, the area beneath them is easier to use than when you let the branches grow almost to ground level. The area beneath the tree can become home to comfortable chairs placed in the shade, an inviting area on hot, humid summer days. You may also plant shrubs or flowers underneath the pruned tree to make your yard more eye-catching and inviting —both to people and to small wildlife like cute little chipmunks.

When using pruning techniques to train a young tree, you'll be avoiding problems that will probably need pruning attention in future years when the tree is grown.

Although you may now think of pruning primarily when faced with rejuvenating an overgrown tree or shrub, it's good to know that proper pruning can also make plants grow more robustly. It's true. You can turn a weak lilac into one that grows vigorously and blooms profusely. And pruning can help prevent troublesome diseases, such as mildew and blackspot on roses, which often appear when the leaves and canes on the bush are too numerous and close together.

You can confidently expect that pruning done in the right way and at the right time will improve the appearance of any plant on your property, a big benefit by itself.

There Is a Better Way

Even with all the advantages pruning confers, it's rarely a homeowner's favorite yard chore. After all, pruning involves sharp tools, and most of us aren't sure we know the best way to prune an overgrown shrub that's beginning to block the view from a window and taking over a walkway. Or maybe, we wonder, if we should prune all our shrubs every year. How do you know when a plant needs pruning and how much should be cut off? So, overwhelmed by unanswered questions and doubts, we ignore overgrown plants when we can, hack back the worst offenders occasionally, or use electric hedge trimmers to trim everything into neat, rounded shapes each spring or fall. We copy what neighbors have done in cutting back their crape myrtles, not knowing if it's correct or not.

None of those strategies work well, so then we complain if our azaleas don't flower the next spring or when many of those trimmed bushes need to be cut back again in just a couple of months. And we're generally dissatisfied with the appearance of our yard because the shrubs and trees don't look as good as they should or as the neighbors' do.

Is there a better way? *Yes!* Take a few minutes to learn when, why, and how to prune. That's the purpose of this guide—showing you, step by easy step, how simple it is to prune so that you improve the appearance and health of your plants and make your yard a standout—while spending less time on the chore.

Once you know the trio of tools you need and the best ways to prune shrubs and trees (which generally won't involve electric hedge shears or cutting shrubs into little round balls), the rest is easy. From that point, we show you the proper time to prune the various shrubs in your yard (hollies will be pruned differently from lilacs and at another time of year). Then look at the specific information you need to prune the majority of plants you grow—deciduous and evergreen trees and shrubs, roses, vines, hedges, and fruits and nuts. We even show how to pinch back annuals, perennials, and houseplants to improve their appearance and growth.

If you have an artistic bent, you'll find out how to combine the science and art of pruning by creating living works of art, such as decorative topiary shapes and espalier, in your yard. (See Chapter 12 for details.) What a delight!

Discovering the ins and outs of pruning the plants you own, and the best time to do that, won't take long, and it won't be difficult. And pruning the right way saves hours—and creates beauty—in the long run. So now's the time to get started in the wonderful world of pruning. Let's go!

CHAPTER 1

Pruning Techniques and Tools

Once you've determined that some of the plants in your yard need to be pruned, it's time to find out what equipment you need to do the job and gain an understanding of what happens when you prune. When you know what to expect each time you prune a certain way, you'll suddenly understand why that overgrown shrub in front of the picture window grows back so quickly when given a trim with electric hedge shears several times a summer. Or why that juniper limb that you cut back by half never sprouted any new growth. As for tools, you don't need very many—unless your property is a large one. But for best results, buy the best you can afford. They'll last a long time and give you better results than cheap tools that may not cut cleanly or easily, especially if you keep them clean, oiled, and sharp.

Tools of the Trade

Homeowners with an average yard often can do all the pruning they need to with just three tools available at any hardware or home store—hand pruners, loppers (also known as lopping shears), and a small pruning saw. Those going in for more extensive pruning—including trees and hedges—may need to add a couple more.

Hand Pruners

First is a pair of hand pruners, which you may already own. If you don't (or if your pair is old and no longer sharp), you'll find plenty to choose from at nurseries and home improvement stores. Don't stint on quality, since this is the one tool that you'll use over and over for years. Pruners are used for cutting stems up to ¾ inch in diameter. They come in two main types, called anvil and bypass. You'll also see ergonomic models of each that require less pressure to work. While these may cost a little more, many homeowners feel that they're more than worth it for the effort they save. If you're left-handed, look for hand pruners made especially for you.

Anvil pruners have a sharp blade that comes down into a flat blade called an anvil. Their main drawback is they may crush a stem instead of cutting it.

Bypass pruners have a sharp blade and a curved anvil. They let you cut very closely but typically work best on branches ½ inch in diameter or smaller.

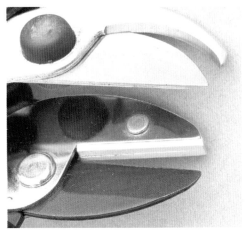

There are two types of hand pruners: bypass, at top, and anvil, at bottom. Use them to cut limbs up to ¾ inch in diameter.

Bypass pruners are the type most recommended by professionals, but try both to see which feels most comfortable and works best in your hand.

Loppers

For cutting stems up to 1¾ inches in diameter, look to long-handled loppers. These may come in anvil and bypass types, as hand pruners do. If so, choose the bypass kind, in order to cut closely inside a large, overgrown shrub. You'll find geared and ergonomic models that give you more cutting power with much less work on your part. These are definitely the way to go.

Pruning Saws

If a limb or stem is too big for loppers (generally up to 5 inches in diameter), then a saw should be able to handle it. The handiest kind to keep around for pruning

Loppers are one of homeowners' most useful pruning tools. Look for models that have cushioned grips and ergonomic gears, which make them much easier to use.

Folding pruning saws are convenient to carry with you in the yard and cut quickly and easily.

is a folding saw (above, right). These are sometimes called Japanese saws. They're useful because they have small teeth, which result in a smoother cut edge. Also, they can be carried in a pocket for use whenever needed. But you can also prune with other saws, if you have them on hand: a double-edge saw (which requires the user to be knowledgeable and very careful) or a bow saw, which, because of its configuration is better for using up in trees than down in shrubs. Long pole saws, used for cutting tall branches while you stand on the ground, are handy when you have many trees that need attention, but expect to practice to learn to use them well. Check to see if you prefer a pole saw that comes in six sections or one that telescopes.

The small, fine teeth on one edge of a double-edge saw are for light trimming. The large teeth on the opposite edge are for cutting thicker limbs.

A bow saw (above) has a lightweight and easy-to-use handle and often an adjustable blade. Pole pruners (at right) let you safely prune branches over your head.

Other Pruning Tools You May Need

Hedge Shears or Hedge Trimmers

If you do a lot of hedge trimming, look for ergonomic models of hedge shears and for types that have notched blades to catch foliage that otherwise might escape. Electric- or gas-powered hedge trimmers make fast work of a long hedge that needs pruning four or five times a year. Just remember: use power hedge trimmers *only* on hedges, not to prune anything else, because of the way they cut. (Read more about this in Chapter 5.)

Chain Saw

If you already have a chain saw, it can be useful for tree pruning. A lightweight 12- or 14-inch model is best for most yards. But it's certainly not necessary to buy one unless you plan extensive tree pruning. A gas model may be safer than an electric model that trails a cord, which can get in the way.

While all of these useful tools are available by mail order, you'll be much happier with the results if you first handle any pruning tool you're thinking of buying. Some may feel too stiff or too heavy or just don't fit your hands comfortably. Don't settle for that. Keep looking locally until you find tools that work well for you. Even people who have arthritic joints will now find ergonomic pruning tools that make the job comfortable for them.

Care of Pruning Tools

Like most common tools, pruning equipment will perform best and last longer if it receives regular TLC. This includes the following:

• Remove excess dirt and debris from tools before putting them away for the day. The easiest way to do this is to use a clean plastic scrubber (commonly sold for kitchen use), warm water, and a small amount of dishwashing soap. After rinsing, dry all parts of the tool.

• Use a light oil (such as 3-in-1) to lubricate as needed. Heavy oils can damage shrub branches or rose canes.

• Unless you have a whetstone and are experienced at using it, let a professional sharpen your tools once a year (late fall is a good time to do it). If you don't know

Manual hedge trimmers are ideal for trimming broadleaf evergreen shrubs since they won't cut leaves in half, as powered hedge trimmers often do.

A lightweight gas chain saw that's 12 to 14 inches long is best for general-purpose yard pruning. On electric models, the cord can get in your way.

Because pruning can cut you as well as branches and, if you make a mistake, a branch can easily fall and damage a car or a person, it's important to observe a few simple safety rules when you prune.

- Protective clothing is a must—long sleeves, long pants, sturdy gloves, safety goggles, and leather shoes or boots that have rubber soles. Add a hard hat if you're cutting tree limbs that are over your head and ear plugs when using a chain saw.
- Never prune alone if you're climbing on a ladder. Have a helper on the ground.
- Use a strong ladder that's placed firmly against a tree so that neither its top nor feet vibrate. It isn't safe to stand on a chair to prune.
- Look above and around where you'll be pruning so you avoid any obstructions, especially power lines (make sure there's no chance you might accidentally cut into electric lines or cause a limb fall on them).
- Be especially cautious with chain saws. Read the direction booklet if you haven't used the saw for some time and follow instructions carefully. Don't lift a chain saw over your head to cut, and be ready for possible kickback.
- When working with large trees, take time in the beginning to evaluate if this may be a job for an experienced professional. Both the International Society of Arboriculture (www.isa-arbor.com) and the National Arborists (www.natlarb.com) can help you find a local tree service. Make sure the company you hire is knowledgeable and fully insured.

anyone who sharpens tools, ask at a hardware store or a shop that services lawn mowers.

- It's especially important to have a knowledgeable person sharpen a pruning saw because this involves "setting" the blade in a certain way, as well as sharpening it. Unless you have a large property and use your saw regularly, it may not need to be sharpened yearly. But do clean, oil, and hang it up after each use.

- If any of your tools have wooden handles, sand off any rough spots when they happen and either oil or varnish the wood as needed.

What Happens During Pruning?

Although you may prefer to skip over this section, it's important for homeowners to understand why plants react the way they do when they grow and they're pruned. Terms such as *apical dominance* and *terminal buds* may make your eyes glaze over, but knowing what happens during pruning tells you why the branch of an evergreen tree won't grow back if you cut it off where there are no needles or why it isn't a good idea to trim shrubs with hedge shears.

First, you'll want to know that plants have different types of buds. Buds are dormant shoots that can eventually produce

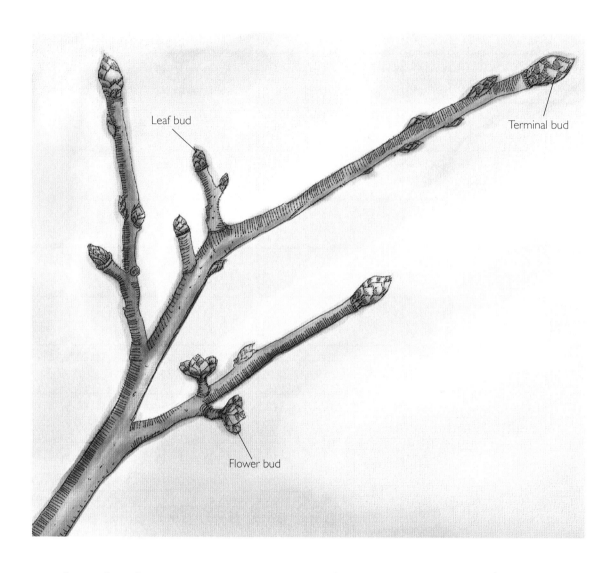

Leaf bud

Terminal bud

Flower bud

leaves, fruit, flowers, or stems. Most won't do anything unless damage or pruning spurs them into action. Sometimes this action isn't what you want. Let's see why.

Terminal buds—those at the end of a stem or branch—exercise dominance over lateral buds—the ones farther down on the sides of the stem—in something called ***apical dominance.*** When you cut off terminal buds—as happens when you shear a shrub all over, cutting all the stems about the same amount—those buds are not in charge and the lateral buds below (usually within 6 to 8 inches of the cut) begin to grow. They produce two or more stems, where before there was just one. If you want to increase branching on a young shrub, this may be the result you desire. However, if you're trying to make a shrub smaller, removing the terminal bud and increasing the number of new stems or branches isn't what you want to happen, because you'll have to prune more frequently to keep the shrub in shape.

Lateral buds may be leaf buds or flower buds that grow along the stem. If you've ever wondered how to tell the difference, flower buds are the ones that are fatter and more of a round shape.

Latent buds are those that are inactive and are found beneath the surface of the bark. Often they're small and not very noticeable. Latent buds, if present, will become active if the terminal bud is cut off the tip of the branch. But many evergreens and some older plants don't have any latent buds on the interior portions of branches or stems. You can tell because the branch has no green growth in that area. Brown needles on a limb mean no latent buds can grow. So pruning on those plants cuts only into green wood that does have latent buds that will sprout.

Later in the book when we talk about pruning various types of plants, you may also want to be familiar one more type of bud: *adventitious buds* often grow in unexpected places, including on roots. They generally appear after pruning or damage has occurred and help produce new branches. But because they come from near a plant's surface, they may cause undesired water sprouts. (See page 62.)

Types of Pruning and What They're Used For

Knowing about the various buds on trees, shrubs, and other plants and how they react when damaged or pruned helps you see what happens when you use one of the various types of pruning. Each style produces a different result and is useful for various types of plants and for different effects.

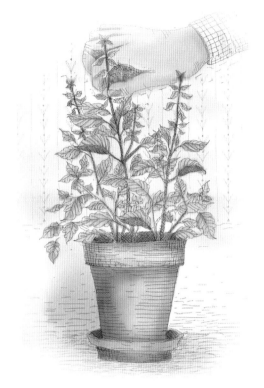

Pinching

Pinching is the simplest pruning style. It rarely needs any equipment and is often done on the spur of the moment when the gardener sees the need or has the time. Pinching is removing the tip of new growth with the thumb and forefinger. Pinching, which removes the terminal bud, results in denser growth on houseplants, herbs, annual and perennial flowers, and some vegetables. On chrysanthemums, it prevents flowers from appearing in summer instead of in fall. With herbs, pinching slows or prevents flowering and keeps the plant producing aromatic leaves and stems longer. Pine trees grow more densely when new growth, or candles, are pinched in half by hand in late spring.

Heading is cutting back, with pruners or loppers, to a random spot on a stem. Because you've removed the terminal bud, vigorous new growth will appear just *below* the new cut. This may be helpful on small shrubs on which you want to encourage new growth and with perennial plants. Think of it as slightly more aggressive pinching. It's not the best overall technique for shrubs because the new growth prevents light from getting into the interior of the plant; all the leaves and growth will be on the exterior of the plant, with nothing on the inside to support it.

Lateral pruning is a type of heading that cuts back a stem or branch to just above a lateral bud. Professional arborists often use this technique to reduce the canopy of a street tree or one growing near power lines or other obstacles. When using lateral pruning on shrubs, always cut to right above a bud that faces the direction toward which you'd like the new growth to go.

Heading

Lateral pruning

Shearing is familiar to anyone who's ever had a hedge. It's also regularly practiced with topiary and bonsai. All stems are cut back about the same amount. Shearing is usually performed with electric or manual hedge shears. Because all the stems are cut to the same length, it produces a formal look (and destroys a shrub's natural shape). For appearance's sake, shearing also needs to be repeated frequently during the growing season. Sheared shrubs with large leaves will look better if care is taken to see that leaves aren't sheared in half. Even more so than with heading, all growth accumulates on the outside of a sheared shrub, preventing light from reaching the interior, eventually killing all growth there. One reason you

Shearing

don't want that to happen is that in case of any injury to the exterior of the shrub (excess snow damage, for instance), there's nothing inside the plant that can sprout and grow. Also, different shrubs have different growth habits. (No one is going to mistake an exuberant, yellow-flowering forsythia for a small, evergreen boxwood, for instance.) These different looks add interest to your yard. If you shear all your shrubs into round balls, your yard won't be as interesting and will appear monotonous.

Thinning reduces the size of a plant while generally maintaining its natural shape. It also doesn't encourage vigorous regrowth that must be cut off again soon. And it keeps the interior of the plant open to sunlight, so it continues actively growing. This is an ideal way to gradually reduce the size of an overgrown shrub without having it look awful for a time (as it would if you cut it half or all the way to the ground). To thin a plant, use pruners, loppers, or a pruning saw to cut back a stem or branch all the way to its base, where it joins the trunk or another stem. Or you can thin by cutting a branch or stem back to the ground.

A crowded shrub is thinned so that it will grow and bloom better, as well as fit better into its location.

How Much Is *Too* Much Pruning?

Trees, shrubs, and other plants are living things—and they can be killed if you prune them too much. The general rule for shrubs is not to prune off more than one-third at a time. It's true that some shrubs can be cut back to the ground and will vigorously and quickly regrow. But delicate shrubs, those that have been damaged, and those that are older may simply die if overpruned. Give young trees 5 or 6 years to grow after planting before removing all branches within 6 or 7 feet of the ground and removing excess growth. As with shrubs, old trees and those in poor health will respond better to gentle pruning spread over several years rather than sudden, severe pruning.

A FEW TIPS ON PRUNING

While we will cover step-by-step directions in the coming chapters for how to prune almost any kind of plant in your yard, here are a few general tips to keep in mind:

- Always make sure that your pruning tools are sharp and clean before you start.
- Know what you want to accomplish before you start to prune—and how to prune to accomplish that goal.
- On shrubs, make your cuts at a 45-degree angle if possible. The reason is that flat cuts may collect water and rot the cut stem. Also, make the cut about ¼ inch above a bud that's facing the way you want the new growth to go. That way, your bush doesn't grow in an unwanted direction and need pruning again before long.
- When pruning trees, never leave a stub (sometimes called a "hatrack"). A stub not only doesn't look good and isn't useful, but it leaves a place for insects or disease to enter the plant.
- Few trees or shrubs—with the exception of fruits—need pruning annually. If you have a shrub or tree that needs to be cut back each year lest it grow too big, it's planted in the wrong spot, one that's too small for it, and you should consider moving it and planting something that grows the right size for the area. Exceptions would be butterfly bush and lilac, which bloom better when pruned yearly. Ornamental grasses also need to be cut back each year.
- If you're pruning a diseased plant, remove all the damaged wood and cut back into good, healthy wood. Remove the diseased wood from the garden immediately. Disinfect your pruners with Lysol or alcohol between cuts.

As you'll learn as you read on through this guide, pruning isn't a mystery or anything to be intimidated by. Once you've chosen the tools you'll need and know what it means to thin a shrub, head one back, or cut off a terminal bud, you're ready to get started pruning hedges, shrubs, trees, and whatever else in your landscape would look better if it were trimmed correctly. One other important piece of knowledge—when to prune and how often—is covered in the next chapter.

CHAPTER 2

When, How Much, and How Often to Prune

Did you know that fall is the wrong time of year to prune just about anything in your yard? That if you trim evergreen azaleas all summer to keep them in a rounded shape, the shrubs will have fewer flowers the next spring? (That's because the flower buds are developing over summer, and you're cutting them off.) In a cold climate, pruning too late in summer can not only banish spring flowers but also subject a shrub to damage from cold weather. In pruning, you see, timing matters. Homeowners need to think not only about the how-to of pruning but also the when-to.

For example, when pruning an azalea or other spring-flowering shrubs, wait until just after flowering has stopped. Then you won't be snipping off developing flower buds. But when do you do prune late-summer bloomers such as butterfly bush or roses that may flower into October or November? Don't worry—we'll help you figure it all out.

How Often Do I Prune Plants?

It's impossible to say specifically how often a shrub, tree, or vine might need to be pruned. Plants will grow faster, and need pruning more often, in warm climates than in cold climates. Young plants will need to be pruned more frequently than old ones. Evergreens need less pruning than shrubs and trees that lose their leaves in fall. Hedges require pruning frequently during the growing season. So do plants that have grown out of bounds where they're growing but need to be keep in that spot. You'll have noticed that some types of plants grow faster than others. A few of the shrubs in your yard may be pruned yearly and others, never. Except in the case of a plant that's overgrown—where the problem and answer are obvious—knowing how often to prune means paying attention to the shrubs and trees in your yard. Ask yourself: How do they look today, as opposed to last year or 2 years before that? If they're not as good, could pruning help make a difference?

How Much Should I Prune Plants?

The first rule of pruning is to prune *only* when a particular plant needs it. Only then do you decide how much needs to be removed—and whether that should be done all at once or over a period of 3 or 4 years.

Trees, shrubs, and other plants are living things—and they can be killed if you prune them too much. **The general rule for shrubs is not to prune off more than one-third at a time.** It's true that some vigorously growing shrubs such as forsythia can be cut back to the ground and will quickly regrow. But boxwood treated the same way will languish. Delicate shrubs, those that have been damaged or are in poor health, and those that are older may simply die if pruned too much or if too much of the plant is removed at one time. Give young trees 5 years to grow after planting before beginning to remove all branches within 6 or 7 feet of the ground and pruning away excess growth. But you'll also want to be cautious when pruning older trees that may not quickly bounce back from too much trimming at one time.

Most plants react better to light pruning than they do to very heavy pruning. Until you know how a particular plant responds to pruning, it's best to err on the side of caution, especially if you don't want to lose the plant. However, if you're ready to remove the overgrown shrub from the yard and you're giving it one last chance, feel free to cut it back severely to see if that rejuvenates it. If it dies, you've learned something and it's no loss. (See pages 31–33 for more about rejuvenation of overgrown shrubs.) For overgrown trees, consider talking with a professional arborist about what steps he or she might be able to take to lessen the size of a tree that's too big or in the way.

When Should I Prune Plants?

On the opposite page is a seasonal checklist that notes the best times to prune various types of flowering shrubs, trees, roses, and vines.

When to Prune Is Critical

Knowing when to prune is critical; you can prune off the best parts if you prune at the wrong time. Prune these shrubs, trees, and vines shortly *after* they finish flowering, so you won't remove the buds that produce next year's flowers.

Shrubs: Azalea, beauty bush, broom, camellia, daphne, deutzia, forsythia, heather, Japanese pieris, Japanese quince, jasmine, kerria, leucothoe, lilac, magnolia shrubs that lose their leaves in winter, mock orange, mountain laurel, pyracantha, rock rose (*Cistus*), serviceberry, rhododendron, viburnum, Virginia sweetspire, weigela, witch hazel, and yucca.

Trees: Carolina silverbell, crab apple, flowering cherry, fringe tree, Japanese quince, deciduous magnolias (those that lose their leaves over winter), ornamental pear trees including Bradford pear, princess

---

For Best Results: Pruning Timing Checklist

Early Spring
- All roses except climbers and ramblers (see more on page 84).
- Summer-flowering shrubs that bloom on new growth (stems or branches that have grown in the current season; aka "new wood"), including beautyberry, bluebeard, butterfly bush, Carolina allspice, crape myrtle, deciduous holly shrubs, flowering maple, fothergilla, Japanese barberry, PeeGee hydrangea (see page 35), redosier dogwood, rose of Sharon, smokebush, summersweet, and witch hazel.
- Vines such as bittersweet, some kinds of clematis (see pages 94–95), climbing hydrangea, creeping fig, cross vine, glory bower, star jasmine, trumpet creeper, variegated kiwi vine (*Actinidia kolomikta*) and wintercreeper.

Late Spring
- All shrubs or trees that have bloomed that spring and need pruning. It's best to do this immediately. Wait no longer than 4 weeks after flowering has finished. That's when new flower buds will have begun to develop.
- New vines; cut them back by one-half when planting.

Summer
- Climbing roses and ramblers that are more than 3 years old (see page 84).
- Trim other types of roses as you cut the flowers.
- Shear privet and other hedges as needed. Stop by mid- or late August.

Fall
- Extra-long rose canes that might whip around in the wind and damage the bush.

Late Winter
- Deciduous trees (except those that bleed; see the box on page 31).
- Fruit trees, vines, and bushes.
- Berried bushes and trees such as evergreen and deciduous holly, nandina, and pyracantha (cut them during December so you can use their branches for holiday decorations).

tree, serviceberry (both tree and shrub forms), and redbud.

Vines: Bougainvillea, Carolina jessamine, some clematis (see pages 94–95), trumpet and goldflame honeysuckle, and jasmine.

To have consistently good results at pruning, it's a good idea to pay attention to a few of the don'ts of pruning:

• Don't prune too late in summer or even in fall because portions of your shrub, tree, or vine, or even occasionally, the entire plant, could be killed back.

• Don't prune off the flower buds before they can open, or you won't have many, if any, blossoms.

Some plants are tough and can withstand heavy pruning, but mostly you'll want to be cautious and not cut too much at one time from most shrubs. That helps them recover faster and grow better. Avoiding these "do nots" will make you more successful at pruning favorite shrubs such as lilac and butterfly bush, which are covered in more detail in the next chapter.

PRUNE THESE TREES IN SUMMER, NOT WINTER

Most deciduous trees—those that lose their leaves in fall—are pruned in later winter, when they're dormant. Exceptions are deciduous trees that also flower (see page 65). But there's a small group of trees that are pruned in the heat of summer. Why? Because when they're pruned in winter's chill, the sap "bleeds" down the trunk, making the tree look as though it's in distress. This really isn't harmful, but most people don't like the look of sap rolling down the side of a tree, sometimes attracting insects. To avoid bleeding, prune these trees in early summer, after weather has warmed up.

River birch

Black locust

Box elder

Dogwood

Elm

Maple

Yellowwood

Walnut

The best time to prune a Kousa dogwood (above) is soon after it finishes blooming. Pruning in late winter will remove many of the flowers —and beauty—that the tree normally produces in late spring or early summer. River birches (at left) tend to "bleed" sap when pruned in winter. Although that doesn't harm the tree, it looks bad and attracts insects. To avoid those problems, wait until summer to trim river birches.

CHAPTER 3

How to Prune Forsythia, Lilac, and Other Deciduous Shrubs

Deciduous shrubs, which lose their leaves each fall and grow new ones in spring, are the most common bushes in the United States. They're the stalwarts of yards in cold-winter climates and familiar as easy-to-grow shrubs by homeowners everywhere, even if we may not know their names: the bright "yellow bells" of forsythia appearing while weather's still chilly to announce that spring's on its way; the readily recognized series of pristine white blooms marching up and down the weeping stems of bridal wreath spirea; the sweet fragrance of lilac that reminds many an adult of spring afternoons in his or her grandmother's garden; the big pink or blue blooms of hydrangea that flop over the big summer leaves; and in the South, crape myrtle that produces bloom after brightly colored bloom from May often until September. And pruning is the key to keeping this oh-so-useful and appealing group of shrubs looking its best.

Start Right, End Right

Your first job is to decide what you want to accomplish by pruning a particular shrub. Do you need a bushier shrub, one that's more compact, one that produces more flowers and blooms longer, a shrub that's larger or smaller than it currently is, a shrub with an attractive natural shape?

A few deciduous bushes (such as bush cinquefoil, forsythia, Japanese quince, and sweetshrub) get messy looking, with tangled growth, unless they're thinned every few years. Several (see the list on page 33) need suckers removed regularly in summer. Otherwise, they'll spread too widely. (You can find out how to do this on page 20.)

When to Prune Flowering Deciduous Shrubs

After you've decided *why* you're pruning, think about timing. Usually, you think of pruning shrubs after they have flowered. But with deciduous shrubs, that's not always true. It depends on when the bush blooms. For spring-flowering deciduous shrubs that flower on what's called old wood, it's simple to know when to prune—do it just after the flowers fade. That gives the plant plenty of time to develop flower buds on the stems that grow all summer after the old ones were trimmed back. On the other hand, summer-flowering shrubs, such as butterfly bush and stewartia, typically bloom on the current year's wood and therefore are

Severely pruning butterfly bush in early spring encourages it to grow many new limbs, which produce more flowers. Without cutting back, the shrub wouldn't bloom very much.

pruned in early spring, before the shrub begins growing, to encourage lots of new growth on which flowers will appear.

Summer-Flowering Shrubs That Are Pruned in Early Spring

- Beautyberry
- Bluebeard
- Bottlebrush buckeye
- Butterfly bush
- Crape myrtle (in warm climates, mid-spring is better for climates where the shrub is marginally hardy)
- Flowering maple (all types of flowering maple except *Abutilon vitifolium,* which is pruned after flowering)
- Lespedeza (in warm climates only; wait until spring in cold-winter areas)
- Pomegranate
- Rose-of-Sharon
- St. John's wort
- Stewartia
- Summersweet
- Sweet shrub (Carolina allspice)

When to Prune Other Deciduous Shrubs

The best time to prune shrubs that aren't grown for their flowers can vary. (Some shrubs do flower, a bit, but they're insignificant and not really considered a flowering shrub.) Check this list to see when to prune the shrubs in your yard.

Late Winter

- Privet

Early Spring

- Burning bush
- Deciduous holly
- Japanese barberry
- Smoke bush
- Staghorn sumac

Late Winter or Early Spring

- Cotoneaster
- Northern bayberry

Spring (after last frost and before summer begins)

- Spicebush

How to Prune Deciduous Shrubs

You'll use your hand pruners for most of the cutting you do on deciduous shrubs. Loppers will come in handy for the thicker stems of mature shrubs, and when it comes to rejuvenating overgrown shrubs, you'll probably want to pull out a pruning saw too.

It's best to wait until shrubs have been in your yard at least 3 years before doing any pruning other than cutting out dead or damaged stems. Even then, prune only when it's needed for one of the reasons we've already

Here's how the base of a butterfly bush could look after the shrub's annual spring trimming. Such drastic pruning looks a bit scary, but the results will wow you in midsummer, when the bush is big and bushy and covered with colorful flowers.

mentioned. That is, prune to make a shrub look better, flower more, and stay the size you need. Otherwise, there's no need to get out the hand pruners or lopping shears. Leave the shrub alone to grow naturally.

Look at your shrub before you start pruning to get a good idea of its normal shape. Cutting all your shrubs back into little round balls (often derisively called meatballs or lollipops by horticulturists) with pruning shears doesn't promote a natural look—and it isn't good for the shrub either. So aim for the natural growth habit of the shrub. It may be upright, spreading, weeping, oval, rounded, or prostrate (creeping low to the ground).

If you have a variegated shrub, one with leaves that are more than one color, you may find that occasionally those leaves will revert to green and whole branches will be covered with green leaves instead of the variegated foliage you expect. One way to take care of the problem is to thin back to the main stem or the ground all stems or branches that have only or mostly green leaves. Do this as soon as you notice the absence of variegation. If you leave the all-green stems on too long, these stronger stems will begin to take over.

Remove suckers in summer (see the accompanying list of shrubs that often sucker) and remove dying or diseased stems anytime you notice them. All other pruning should follow the timing in the list on page 31. To help reduce the size of a shrub, use loppers or hand pruners to thin stems back to a main branch. For overgrown shrubs, consider the techniques on pages 36–37. Thinning will also allow more light into the interior of a shrub, which can stimulate more flowering.

To encourage thicker growth (especially where the shrub is used to provide privacy), use your hand pruners to head back stems to a healthy, outward-facing bud.

DECIDUOUS SHRUBS THAT OFTEN PRODUCE SUCKERS

Bottlebrush buckeye
Japanese kerria
Lilac
Northern bayberry
Pomegranate
Staghorn sumac
Witch hazel

It's better to let shrubs grow into natural shapes rather than prune them into round balls that concentrate all the growth on the outside of the shrub.

Pruning Hydrangeas

One of the frustrations gardening experts hear most often in late spring and early summer is, "My hydrangea didn't bloom!" The most frequent cause is that the flower buds were killed by late spring frosts. The second most common reason that hydrangeas that are otherwise in good condition haven't flowered is that they've been pruned at the wrong time. Actually, hydrangeas don't really need much regular pruning, except removing dead stems and faded flowers (the latter are often used in dried flower arrangements). But if you do need to prune a hydrangea, deciding when to do it can be confusing because there are several types of hydrangea, and they're pruned at different times. Here's when and how to prune each kind:

How to Prune Hydrangeas

• All hydrangeas: Anytime you notice them, remove weak, dead, or damaged stems and stems that cross and rub. In spring, after new growth is visible, cut out all winter damage, back to the ground or to live wood. In warm climates, remove any flowers that are still on the shrub. In areas with cold winters, leaving the faded flowers on the shrub can protect the flower buds from cold damage. Remove them in spring after new growth begins to appear. If needed, renovate hydrangeas that are more than 5 years old by cutting one-third of the oldest stems back to the ground each year for 3 years. (See page 37 for more about this technique.) Do this in early spring just before growth starts. This technique also increases vigor and works to reduce the size of

WHEN TO PRUNE HYDRANGEAS

Hydrangea arborescens ('Annabelle'; smooth hydrangea)—Early spring, just before new growth starts

Mophead and lacecap hydrangeas—In summer immediately after flowering

Hydrangea quercifolia (oakleaf hydrangea)— Right after flowering

an unruly hydrangea. If a hydrangea has gotten floppy or too loose, cut the floppy stems back to ground level.

• *Hydrangea arborescens* ('Annabelle') and PeeGee hydrangeas: These charming shrubs bloom on new wood, so they can be cut back in late winter or early spring. Many gardeners cut them back to less than a foot tall or even to ground level. The problem with doing that is that it creates new, weaker growth at the top of the plant, which can't support the weight of heavy blossoms, especially Annabelle's. One way to avoid this is to laterally prune (see page 18) the stems about 18 or 24 inches high. This makes the stems sturdier and more able to support heavy flowers. PeeGee hydrangeas may also be pruned in a tree shape.

• Mophead, lacecap, and oakleaf hydrangeas: Remove flowers shortly after they fade. Do this before August in warm climates. In cold climates, remove old blooms in spring, cutting just above a fat, round flower bud. Control shrub size, if necessary, by cutting a few of the older canes back to ground level.

• Everblooming or reblooming hydrangea: These are a bit more difficult to prune because they bloom both on old wood, or stems from a previous season, and also on new wood the plant produces during the current growing season. These two types of flowering usually call for pruning at different times. Don't cut 'Endless Summer' and other everblooming hydrangeas to ground level because you'll be removing the next season's flowers. Wait until after the shrub is at least 2 years old before doing necessary pruning, other than removing dead or diseased stems. Then, when you deadhead

Hydrangea paniculata (PeeGee hydrangea)—Late winter or early spring

Everblooming or reblooming hydrangea ('Endless Summer' series)—After flowers fade and in fall

the flowers, cut them off with a pair of sharp hand pruners to just above the second set of leaves or leaf buds below the flower. Do this before August. Renovate an overgrown everblooming hydrangea by cutting down to ground level one-third of the old stems each year for three years. When you do that, you will lose some of the following year's flowers, but it won't be as noticeable as if you pruned at the wrong time.

How to Rejuvenate an Overgrown Deciduous Shrub

Overgrown shrubs are a common problem. This situation is often caused because someone never thought of pruning to keep the bush at a reasonable size or because a homeowner simply didn't know how to do it. Usually, the person who buys the property next is faced with the question of what to do. By then, a shrub can be *really* overgrown!

Actually, it's not as hopeless as you might think. There are three simple ways to deal with overgrown shrubs. The best time to tackle this job is in early spring because that's when regrowth will be faster.

Take It Slow and Easy

This method is for homeowners who have patience or are working on a shrub in a prominent location in the yard and don't want even a temporary eyesore. What you do is get out your loppers or folding saw and remove one-third of the stems—the biggest ones, if possible—at ground level. Early the next spring (when the weather is still cold, and before most shrubs flower), do the same thing to another one-third of the remaining stems. The third year, remove the final third of the original stems. By the fourth spring, you will have a shrub that is

When shrubs are overgrown, you can start to easily rejuvenate them in late winter by pruning one-third of the oldest stems back to ground level. Do the same thing the next two years.

Years 2 and 3

In the second and third years, again remove to soil level one-third of the older stems.

Year 4

In the fourth year, the shrub will be shorter, smaller, and growing well. It will be the right size for where it's growing.

just the size to fit where it's growing and is a natural shape.

If the shrub you're rejuvenating is old and one you want to be careful with, rejuvenate it over 4 years, instead of 3. (An "old" shrub is one that's totally established, more than 5 years at least.) In year 1, remove one-fourth of the stems; in year 2, remove one-fourth of the remaining stems; and so forth, until all original stems have been removed.

When You Need to Take Drastic Measures

Why not cut down the shrub and see if it will grow back? That's the natural inclination of

Vigorous shrubs that have become overgrown respond well when you cut them back to 6 to 12 inches high. They won't look good for about a year or more, though.

many people who are faced with overgrown shrubs. And actually, it isn't a bad idea—for shrubs that are used to growing vigorously. Check the sidebar at right for a list of shrubs that grow robustly. Some shrubs, particularly old ones, may not respond to such hard treatment, so try this only if you don't care if the bush survives.

Prune That Big Shrub Into a Tree

Another way to make an overgrown shrub look better and fit more attractively into your landscape is to transform it into a tree. This makes a big space difference because the lower stems or trunks will be bare, not taking up as much room in your garden as they did before. The growth will be *up*, not out.

1. Choose three stems in the shrub that will become the new tree's trunks. You'll want them well spaced so they aren't rubbing or crowding one another.

Then cut all other vertical stems down to ground level.

2. Next cut off all the side limbs on each remaining trunk so that the new trunks have no limbs growing on the bottom 5 feet of the trunks. To maintain the tree form, promptly snip off with hand pruners any new growth that appears on the cleared portion of the trunks.

HOW TO PRUNE CLUMPING BAMBOO

If you have running bamboo, which spreads like crazy, it's nearly impossible to get rid of it (or even get it under control) by pruning the top of the plant. However, clumping bamboo is more mild-mannered; its roots are not invasive, although they do spread slowly year by year.

• To prune clumping bamboo, first use a pruning saw to cut back to ground level any yellow or brown stalks or those that are leaning over instead of growing relatively straight. Then do the same thing to older stalks (those that are a deeper or duller green) that are growing too closely to sidewalks, paths, driveways, perennial borders, and so forth.

• Next, cut back up to one-fourth to one-third of older stalks in clumps that are growing too crowded. Cut them just above the third raised ring (or node) from the bottom of the stalk. Be careful not to remove more than a total of one-third of the plant's stalks through pruning each year.

Lilacs are popular for the distinctive fragrance and appearance of their attractive flowers. But when a lilac isn't pruned regularly, there are fewer and fewer flowers, which generally appear only at the top of the shrub.

Pruning a Lilac

When an old-fashioned lilac bush has grown 20 feet tall and has blooms mostly way up at the top and bare lower branches, it needs pruning to return it to its former glory. Here's how:

Prune lilacs immediately after the flowers have faded and fallen off. Thin out all dead or damaged wood in the shrub. Then head back (page 18) branches that have grown out of bounds and interfere with the shape of the shrub. Always cut these at a 45-degree angle just above an outward-facing bud.

Over a period of 3 or 4 years, remove a third or fourth of all stems that are more than 2 inches in diameter by cutting them back to ground level. At the end of that time, your lilac will be rejuvenated and should be blooming well again.

For renewal pruning of a severely overgrown lilac, cut back *half* the oldest, largest stems—spaced evenly through-out the shrub—back to 8 inches tall. This will encourage plenty of new growth. The differences between this technique and cutting back fewer stems over a longer period of time is that this has faster results, but the bush won't look very good for the first 2 years. Gradual renewal yields a more attractive appearance even though you're actively pruning, but it takes longer.

Dwarf Korean lilacs rarely need that much pruning. Often you can keep them under control by removing dead or diseased wood and crossing branches. But if they become larger than wanted, cut them back as you would other lilacs but over 3 or 4 years.

Deciduous shrubs are among the most variable plants in your yard, but they aren't hard to prune. Pay attention to timing and maintaining a natural shape, and you'll do fine. Evergreen shrubs, next, usually can't be cut back as hard as the deciduous shrubs, but they often don't need as much pruning either.

HOW AND WHEN TO CUT BACK ORNAMENTAL GRASSES

Pruning ornamental grasses is a lot like pruning shrubs. If you don't cut back your ornamental grasses each year, new green growth will sparsely grow up among old brown growth—and look awful. So it's important to prune all ornamental grasses (especially the ones as large as shrubs) early each spring. The timing will vary from February in USDA hardiness zone 8 and warmer, March in zones 6 and 7, to after the snow is gone for good in cold climates.

It's easy to trim back smaller grasses with loppers, manual hedge shears, or even hand pruners. But for larger specimens, you'll probably need to use electric hedge shears or a weed-whacker with a metal blade. Always cut larger grasses back to no taller than 6 to 8 inches. Smaller ones can be pruned back to about 3 inches high. For neatness's sake, always remove the dead foliage from the garden. Consider spreading it on a woodland pathway, since it's a natural brown and lasts a long time, even underfoot.

CHAPTER 4

How to Prune an Azalea and Other Broadleaved and Needled Evergreen Shrubs

E vergreen shrubs vary widely in appearance and the qualities they bring to your yard. Quite a few develop lovely flowers—azalea, camellia, rhododendron, and winter daphne among others. Then there are shrubs covered with needles instead of leaves—juniper, mugo pine, and yew. An evergreen shrub can hug the ground or grow taller than 12 feet. A few are thorny and need a careful approach. Others are undemanding. You'll find weeping, upright, round, pyramidal, and spreading shapes. So it's a versatile group, and your goals for pruning will vary, depending on what you grow. For a flowering shrub, you'll want to encourage abundant blooms. On plain evergreens, it's important to maintain the natural shape (by thinning, page 20) and to stimulate bushiness by pinching back tips or lateral pruning (page 18). Sometimes you'll need to control size. And for shrubs harmed by extra-cold winters, you'll want to promptly remove damage and stimulate new growth.

How to Prune Needled Evergreen Shrubs

These techniques are right for evergreen shrubs, which include arborvitae, dwarf false cypress, shorter hemlocks (such as 'Emerald Fountain', 'Gracilis', and 'Sargent's Weeping'), juniper, mugo pine, spruce, and yew. They are the same techniques used for deciduous shrubs.

With all shrubs, your initial attention in pruning is to remove any dying or dead, diseased, or damaged wood when you notice it. Otherwise, your shrub may be subject to insect invasion or disease infestation, and these can spread to other plants in your yard. Although most evergreen shrubs may need very little pruning, it's also important to keep an eye on them and remove branches that cross and rub against each other, or have the potential to rub, removing bark and, again, leaving a point of entry for insects and diseases. At the proper time for pruning your shrub (see page 49), remove these branches by thinning them back even with the trunk, or if the damage is small, cut them back into green wood, just above an obvious bud, if possible. Needled evergreens are notorious for not regrowing when cuts are made into an old, interior part of the branch that no longer has needles, so it's important to remove all of a branch if most of it is damaged, or to cut back no farther than an area that has green needles. Remove all suckers at the base of the shrub (see page 33), and pull out dead needles that interfere with seeing exactly what you need to do to open up the interior to more light.

Thinning (see page 20), which removes a branch or stem, is the preferred technique for pruning needled evergreen shrubs. It will help preserve the shrubs' natural shape at the same time it stimulates the growth of branches, but won't produce the fast, excessive growth that requires you to prune again in a few months.

Heading back (page 18), removal of a portion of a branch, must be used with care on needled evergreens so that you don't end up with a (possibly dead or dying) stub in the middle of the plant.

Lateral pruning (page 18) is better than heading for needled evergreens because it ends just above a noticeable bud from which new growth will appear. This is an especially good technique to use when you're pruning to maintain a pyramidal shape because it directs the growth in a predictable way.

Shearing (page 19) might seem to be the answer for maintaining a natural conical shape of a needled evergreen—and it won't hurt to do it once every few years—but shearing causes new growth to build up on the tips of the stems, concentrating new growth on the outside of the shrub instead of throughout the plant, which is healthier. But if you prefer to shear, evergreen shrubs that tolerate it well are boxwood and yew in addition to hedges of arborvitae and hemlock.

Shearing an evergreen shrub

Heading back an evergreen shrub

Lateral pruning an evergreen

How to Prune a Creeping Juniper and Other Creeping Needled Evergreens

As the name makes clear, creeping junipers (and other creeping needled evergreens, such as Siberian cypress) like to spread, making them useful as an excellent and tough groundcover. But when these junipers grow too close to a sidewalk, path, or street, they're usually just hacked back from the protruding edges, leaving large areas of big brown branches visible. So proper planting makes a great deal of difference if you have to prune these popular shrubby groundcovers much. The other issue with creeping junipers is that growth becomes too dense as they become older, which can lead to insect and disease problems as well as interior dieback of needles.

First, you want to be sure that your creeping juniper is in full sun. If it isn't, the plant is going to gradually decline, no matter what, and pruning only postpones the inevitable.

Then thin (page 20) dead or damaged branches and some of the top branches in the center to avoid having them completely shade the branches below.

Also thin (cut back to the branch's end or to where it joins another branch) overlapping branches and those that are growing out of bounds. With thinning cuts, you won't end up with those ugly brown stems prominently in view.

Using lateral pruning (page 18), cut back the side branches to reduce the shrub's size. Keep lateral cuts back in the greenery so the cut brown branch ends won't be so visible.

Creeping junipers usually have at least some buds where there are no needles growing on the interior part of the branch nearest the main trunk, which means that you may be able to prune them farther back than other evergreens. However, this practice is often iffy, so it's best not to cut back into branches that don't have green needles on them, unless it's necessary.

Prune creeping junipers subtly in their interior to keep them in bounds. Whacking creeping junipers back when they reach the curb ruins their appearance.

Pruning Broadleaved Evergreens

As with needled shrubs, broadleaved evergreens, if planted in the right spot, may never need pruning, which is a joy. But when one does get out of bounds a bit or develops dead stems that need to be removed, you'll find the job is easy since broadleaf evergreens are pruned much like deciduous shrubs. Since this group of shrubs includes those that produce decorative berries as well as flowers, you'll want to think about the right time of year to prune.

Flowering shrubs are usually best pruned right after their flowers fade. (Don't wait too long, or buds for next year's blossoms will be forming and you'll cut them off as you prune.) Prune berried shrubs in late

Don't cut holly back into the part of the stem that doesn't have any green leaves on it. No new regrowth will resprout.

winter or early spring (after the migrating birds have enjoyed the bounty, if possible). For other shrubs, check our list (see page 49) to be sure, but generally you can't go wrong with pruning in late winter or early spring before new growth has begun.

Follow the directions for pruning deciduous shrubs (Chapter 3), but *always* avoid shearing broadleaf evergreens with large leaves (rhododendrons, pieris, tea olive, mahonia, and so forth) because using hedge shears on those shrubs tears the leaves and makes them look unattractive, especially when viewed up close. Exceptions are small-leaved shrubs, such as boxwood, that are sheared in a hedge. But when they're grown as individual shrubs in your yard, prune them by thinning, heading back, and lateral pruning (pages 18-20). Use thinning to control a shrub's size, to encourage more flowering, and to remove leggy branches. Heading back will help the shrub develop thicker growth where needed.

BROADLEAF EVERGREENS YOU SHOULD NOT HEAD BACK

Avoid cutting these broadleaf evergreen shrubs back into old or bare growth, because they will not resprout with new growth. The result is a hatrack, or portion of a branch that is bare. This problem occurs with almost all needled evergreens but also for those broadleaf evergreen shrubs listed below. Always thin these shrubs instead. (See the directions on page 20.)

Bottlebrush

Heather

Holly

Nandina

Rock rose

Tea tree

Rejuvenating a Broadleaved Evergreen Shrub

Although many broadleaf evergreens grow slowly, others expand vigorously and some become too large because they've been neglected. If you're faced with the job of renovating a broadleaf evergreen, the best way to do it is to thin out one-third or one-fourth of the oldest branches over 3 or 4 years. The longer time is best for old shrubs and those that aren't in tip-top shape. You can even stretch the process to 5 years, if you like. (Read all about this process and see the drawings illustrating how to do it on page 37.) At the end of the period, your shrub will look new, be a smaller size, have a natural form, and be covered with lots of healthy new growth. (This is also an excellent way to keep barberries in shape.)

Whatever you do, avoid the temptation to hack back all your overgrown evergreens about a half or third from the top with loppers or electric shears. It will look awful, the new growth may be produced too fast and not in the areas you need it (requiring you to prune again before long), and—most important—if

you prune back into areas that don't have any leaves, the stem or branch probably won't resprout; it will stay bare. That's not the result you want.

However, a few vigorous broadleaf evergreens may be cut back hard, if needed, during renovation. Check out the list above of those plants.

EVERGREEN SHRUBS THAT WILL TOLERATE HARD PRUNING

Aucuba
Cotoneaster (upright varieties)
Gardenia (after winter damage)
Glory bower
Glossy abelia
Hebe
Ivy tree
Japanese euonymus
Leatherleaf viburnum
Oleander
Pyracantha
St. John's wort
Sweet box
Thorny elaeagnus
Yew

When evergreen shrubs grow out of bounds, prune them so they're smaller and better fit into the spot where they're planted.

Evergreen shrubs don't share a common time that's best to prune. Instead, check these lists to find when to prune those in your yard.

Late Winter
- Manzanita (regular pruning; pinching is okay in late spring and early summer)

Early Spring
- Boxleaf azara
- Bottlebrush (may also prune after flowering)
- Camellia (after flowering; see box on page 50 for more information)
- Escallonia
- Heath (summer- and fall-flowering varieties only)
- Heather (major pruning; minor pruning is fine after flowering)
- Hebe (may groom in early to midsummer)
- Ivy tree (major pruning; pinch as needed anytime)
- Japanese cleyera (major pruning; can pinch in spring)
- Japanese euonymus (major pruning in warm climates; may trim in late spring or early summer)
- Japanese privet (major pruning; may be groomed anytime needed; hedges are regularly sheared during summer)
- Juniper (best time is when the shrub is dormant, but it may be pruned in early summer or actually anytime)
- Oleander
- Shiny xylosma (major pruning; wait until after flowering to do grooming or shaping)
- Tea tree
- Viburnum (major pruning; wait until after flowering for any minor pruning)

Late Winter or Early Spring
- Aucuba
- Boxwood (regular pruning; may shape anytime)
- Cotoneaster
- Glossy abelia
- Holly
- Nandina (may be pinched in late spring)
- Yew (major pruning; may shear during late spring and summer)

Spring
- Anise
- Cliff green
- Glory bower
- St. John's wort
- Wax myrtle

After Flowering
- Azalea (see page 50 for more information)
- Broom
- Heath (only varieties that flower in winter or spring)
- Japanese pieris
- Leucothoe
- Mountain laurel
- Oregon grape holly (major pruning; light pruning, anytime)
- Pyracantha
- Rhododendron (see page 50 for more information)
- Rock rose
- Thorny elaeagnus
- Tree anemone
- Winter daphne
- Yucca

Other Times
- Australian fuchsia, anytime
- Cherry laurel, anytime
- Gardenia, anytime in frost-free climates; in spring where winters regularly fall below freezing
- Grampian, spring and summer
- Indian hawthorn, spring and summer
- Japanese euonymus, in cold climates, wait to prune until after spring frosts end
- Japanese fatsia, spring or summer
- Japanese pittosporum, anytime
- Loropetalum, after spring flowering
- Mugo pine, late spring or early summer after candles (no growth) have appeared but have not hardened
- Myrtle, anytime
- Photinia, spring through midsummer
- Skimmia, summer
- Sweet box, anytime
- Tea olive, anytime

How to Prune "The Big Three"— Evergreen Azaleas, Camellias, and Rhododendrons

How to Prune Evergreen Azaleas

To control size, thin the plant (page 20) in early spring or after flowering. Remove faded flowers if they don't fall off on their own. (An easy way to do this is to lightly sweep them off with a broom.) Encourage bushier growth by lightly pinching (page 17) the tips of the stems shortly after flowers have faded. Renovate an azalea by cutting one-third of the oldest stems back to 6 inches high each year for 3 years. A few of the toughest azaleas may be cut back to 1 foot high when overgrown and allowed to regrow, but there are no guarantees the plant will recover. Whatever you do, don't shear (or otherwise prune) a spring-flowering azalea in summer. That cuts off the next spring's flowers, and shearing will interfere with the shrub's natural shape.

Encourage bushier growth on evergreen azalea shrubs by lightly pinching the tips right after the flowers have faded.

How to Prune Camellias

If you're growing camellias in an area where they aren't always reliably winter hardy, some experts suggest that it's safest to do major pruning of camellias only in spring, just before new growth begins. The usual advice is that it's okay to prune camellias after flowering, and the best time for fall- or winter-flowering varieties is late winter. It's fine to follow that advice if you're growing camellias in a mild-winter climate. But those in colder or variable climates may lose a recently pruned shrub when it's been cut back not too long before a couple of unexpected spells of lower-than-usual temperatures. Anyone with a spring-flowering camellia will want to prune it just after flowering. When camellias are grown in containers in a greenhouse or indoors, prune them when they're placed outside in spring, because that's when new growth will begin.

Thin (page 20) to increase vertical growth. Light heading back (page 18) will encourage the shrub to grow more branches and become wider. The safest way to renovate a camellia (see 36) is by cutting by one-third of the oldest stems to the ground over 3 years. But if you're willing to take a chance, most can be cut back to 6 inches tall in spring and allowed to regrow. Pinch the tips of the stems (page 17) anytime during the growing season (but stop in August) to encourage bushy growth. When you cut off a camellia blossom to put it in a vase or bowl, remove two or three leaves just below the flower at the same time. This practice helps keep the shrub in shape. If you'd like to try disbudding (page 123) to develop larger, more impressive flowers, camellia is a good shrub to try this on.

To gently renovate a camellia, remove one-third of the stems to ground level each year for 3 years.

How to Prune Rhododendrons

The easiest pruning on a rhododendron—and the one you're likely to do most often—is just maintaining the shrub at its current size and shape. Start by snapping the old flowers off by hand when they've finished blooming. If you can't reach all of the blossoms, try knocking off those out of reach with a strong stream of water or by sweeping them off with a broom. This step matters because you don't want the plant to devote energy trying to produce seeds through those old blooms. Deadheading your rhododendron may also prevent the shrub from blooming every other year instead of yearly.

Just as with azaleas, pinching the tips of rhododendrons' stems will encourage new growth and branches. Wait until the new growth is about 4 inches long, then pinch or cut about one-fourth of it off just above a set of leaves.

Prune rhododendrons right after flowering because the shrubs bloom on old wood. Always remove dead and dying wood first thing if you haven't done so earlier when it appeared.

Rejuvenate rhododendrons by thinning one-fourth of the oldest stems back to 6 inches or ground level after flowering has finished each year for 4 years. This lets more light inside the shrub and encourages new growth.

Evergreen shrubs are valued for providing year-round greenery in our landscapes, and it's hard to imagine any yard without at least one evergreen. They typically don't need much pruning, but it's best to shape an evergreen shrub, needled or broadleaf, when it's young because it becomes much harder to reduce size or correct a poor shape when the shrub is mature.

It's just the opposite with hedges, covered in the next chapter. Year after year, no matter what their age, hedge shrubs are pruned frequently during the growing season. Different plants require differences in pruning techniques and timing. Once you know the reasons for the variances, how to prune each type of plant will become automatic.

As soon as rhododendron flowers have faded, pinch off those you can reach and use a clean broom to sweep off those over your head.

CHAPTER 5

How to Prune a Hedge

A h, hedges, here's something that everyone thinks he or she knows how to prune. And each person is probably right—up to a point. Buy a pair of hedge shears and cut stems back until they're even. But there are tips that even someone who prunes a hedge three or four times yearly might be surprised to learn. Do you know, for instance, which should be wider, the top or bottom of a hedge? And should all hedges be trimmed neatly in a formal look? That's the image most of us have of a hedge, but in reality, hedges can be short or tall; have weeping edges or grow straight up; and be deciduous, flowering, or evergreen. Hedges are used for privacy, blocking unsightly views; as walls, marking a property line; and defining space within the landscape (around an herb garden, for example). Those differences can cause variations in pruning techniques and frequency.

Do You Want a Formal or Informal Style?

Formal hedges, with tops and sides pruned so they're level, are the most popular type.

A formal, tightly pruned hedge will be more work than an informal hedge because it requires more effort to keep it looking as though it should be in a military parade, marching along with precision. This will mean shearing it (see page 19) several times during the growing season. Typical shrubs for formal hedges include arborvitae, aucuba, boxwood, evergreen holly, evergreen privet, Leyland cypress, and yew.

An informal hedge is allowed to grow in its natural shape—if it's a hedge made up of forsythia shrubs, for example, the shrubs will be pruned only to keep the hedge at the size that the homeowner needs, or to remove dead or damaged portions. That's very little work, and for good reason: a forsythia shrub would look silly pruned as a

Informal hedges, such as forsythia, require less work.

boxwood hedge might be—without a leaf out of place—and pruning it that way will prevent it from flowering much, the main reason to grow forsythia. If you want an informal hedge—a good choice with an informal house and landscape—you'll need to see a picture of the mature shrub, if it's unfamiliar, so you know what the natural shape is that you're maintaining.

Start Right in the Beginning

A good-looking and easily pruned hedge starts at planting time. When planting or within a month, head back (see page 18) the stems of all hedge shrubs by about one-third. Yes, it's tough to convince yourself to make smaller all those little shrubs you want to see grow as large as possible as quickly as possible. But if your goal is a dense hedge—and it should be—then pruning in the beginning will make a big difference because it creates many new branches, especially near the base of the hedge where bareness is hard to correct later. If you don't cut back in the beginning, the new branches will be mostly at the top and the growth on the inside of the hedge won't be strong. That's not a good start for any hedge, and it doesn't bode well for long-term success either. The good news is that after the initial pruning, you can wait until the hedge has been in your yard for 2 years before doing any other pruning except removing damaged wood.

Prune formal hedges often in summer so they don't get out of shape.

Pruning Techniques for Formal and Informal Hedges

Shearing

Shearing (see page 19) is the main pruning technique for formal hedges, although any damaged or diseased stems should be removed with hand pruners or loppers. Manual pruning shears are fine for small hedges (and those gardeners who like to get a workout in the yard rather than at the gym). They have a big advantage over power pruning shears because they allow the person doing the pruning to maintain better control.

One big problem with electric pruners is that they cut leaves in half or thirds instead of leaving them whole. This isn't especially noticeable on needled evergreens or hedge shrubs that have small leaves. But it doesn't look good on hedges with larger leaves, such as some privets or hollies. It destroys the neat look that you've worked so hard to create. If the appearance of the cut leaves bothers you, but you want to use electric pruning shears because of their speed, go back and cut off the damaged leaves with hand pruners.

Informal Hedges

Informal hedges are pruned much like the individual shrubs that make up the hedge. That is, a rhododendron hedge is pruned much like an individual rhododendron in your yard and at the same time. Instead of shearing informal hedges with hedge shears (which will give them a uniform appearance), use

Electric- or gas-powered hedge trimmers make quick work of pruning a hedge.

thinning cuts (see page 20) to make sure they don't grow out of bounds and that they don't grow so thick that sunlight doesn't reach in the insides of the plants.

Safety First

For safe pruning, don't use electric hedge shears in damp weather. Also be careful to wear long sleeves and pants, closed-toe shoes, and heavy gloves. Make sure that stepladders are stable. If possible, have someone with you to hold a ladder in place. Never hold power pruners over your head when pruning.

TAPER, TAPER, TAPER FORMAL HEDGES

When you look at formal hedges that have recently been sheared, most look as though they have straight sides to go with a level top. That may be how many of us think a formal hedge should look. But actually, we're wrong. The sides should be tapered a bit so that the bottom of the hedge is slightly wider than the top. The bottom wider than the top? Yes. If the top is wider than the base—as usually happens—it blocks the sun from reaching the bottom growth, which then loses its leaves and becomes bare. That unfortunate occurrence detracts from the look of the entire hedge and isn't always easy to correct later. To trim a hedge so that the bottom is wider than the top, begin your shearing at the bottom of the hedge, instead of at the top, and taper the sides as you work your way up.

Correct hedge pruning

Incorrect hedge pruning

Formal hedges should be pruned so they're wider at the bottom than the top. Otherwise, the bottom of the hedge is shaded and won't grow or look good.

How Often Should You Prune a Hedge?

For a formal hedge, get out the shears whenever there's about 3 inches of new growth. Mature informal hedges—those older than 3 years—will need thinning about once yearly, enough to keep them in shape and from growing too large. This can be done anytime during the year that's recommended for the kind of shrub that makes up your hedge, typically from late winter through spring but after flowering for blooming hedges. Prune evergreens in mid-spring. Remove all dead or damaged stems and trim out crowded growth that mars the appearance of the hedge.

When to stop? Many gardeners stop pruning hedges in August or early September because newly pruned shrubs

Give a fast-growing hedge its first trimming of the season when there's 3 or 4 inches of new growth. Prune a slow-growing hedge after the first flush of growth is complete.

are more sensitive to damage from cold weather; ending then protects their hedge. The exact timing depends on where you live, but you should be fine if you do your last hedge pruning at least 6 to 8 weeks before the average first fall frost in your area. (Your local Extension service office can tell you this date, if you don't know it.)

How to Renovate a Neglected Hedge

If you've moved to a property with a hedge that's been neglected and you'd like to restore and keep it, it can usually be renovated if it isn't diseased and it receives enough sunlight. You'll need some patience, though. Renovation may take several years, and the hedge may not look very good (or provide any privacy) during that time. Still, it may be easier to renovate an established hedge than to plant a new one. And it's much less expensive.

Another reason to renovate a hedge is because the entire bottom section is bare, which isn't going to improve on its own.

The first step in renovation is probably the hardest. Go through the hedge and remove all plants that aren't part of the hedge. These are little weed plants that have sprung up at the bottom of the hedge, often from seeds dropped by birds. (You can distinguish them because they have different leaves and a different growth habit than the regular hedge plants.) Cut them down as far as you can and then dig them out by the roots, if possible.

Next, in spring before new growth starts, you have a couple of choices of how to proceed.

Some vigorously growing hedge plants can be cut to about a foot above the ground and allowed to regrow. Aucuba, euonymus, camellia, many hollies, privet, spirea, and viburnum fall into this category. (Boxwoods may or may not recover from such treatment, so it isn't recommended unless you're willing to deal with them not growing back at all.)

For other hedge plants, you'll want to take the 3- or 4-year renovation approach described in the chapter about pruning deciduous shrubs (see page 28). Remove one-third of the older stems at their base each year for 3 years, and at that point you will have what's basically a new hedge, one that looks great.

Most homeowners consider pruning a hedge an easy DIY project—and it is, even though it requires pruning more often than anything else in your yard. But what about trees, in the next chapter? Is cutting a storm-damaged limb off a large maple tree also something that's simple to do yourself? Or is this larger project something you hire a professional to do? Even if it's the latter, you need to know the correct way so you can see if it's been done right and will result in a healthy tree that continues growing well.

CHAPTER 6

How to Prune Dogwoods, Maples, and Other Deciduous Trees

E veryone loves trees. Maples enrich fall days with orange and red leaves that are too bright to be ignored. Sturdy, tall oaks provide shelter and food for squirrels and other small wildlife. The pristine flowers of flowering dogwood, linden, and tulip poplar enhance spring and summer yards. In return for the shade and beauty these popular deciduous trees provide year after year, they sometimes need pruning to improve their health, lengthen their lives, and make them safer for the people who live around them. Pruning a tree is more than lopping off the ends of branches. In fact, that's the wrong thing to do. The right thing isn't difficult, but before you start, think about the size of the tree needing work. If it's quite large or storm-damaged, this might be the time to call in an expert, instead of doing it yourself. To help you decide, see Safety First on page 15.

An Ounce
of Prevention

Since pruning a large, mature tree can be quite a job—and it takes some time for the tree to recover—it's good to know that maintenance pruning and training young trees (page 67) can help you prevent much pruning on established trees.

The first step in all pruning is to remove, through thinning (page 20), damaged, dead, or diseased branches, or those that have become home to insects. That's good maintenance. It can be done anytime during the year, but winter is excellent. When you're dealing with a diseased limb, always disinfect your saw with Lysol between cuts. If the branch is large and heavy, the instructions

When cutting off a tree limb, don't cut flush with the trunk. Instead, cut into the branch collar, where the branch joins the trunk or another large limb.

and illustrations on page 66 will show you how to proceed. On young trees, cut the branch back to the trunk, using a pruning saw. Don't leave a stub because that can cause insect or disease damage and lead to rotting. You also want to avoid cutting flush with the trunk and into what's called the branch collar. (See the photo below.) There's no need to apply wound dressing of any sort after removing a limb from a tree. Scientific studies have shown that it generally doesn't help.

The second part of maintenance pruning is to remove one branch whenever two cross or rub each other. The problem will only get worse as the limbs grow larger.

Next, look for suckers at the base of trees. These are small, weak growths that emerge from the roots. They steal water and nutrients from the tree and contribute nothing to it. Some trees develop suckers regularly, others don't. But when there are many of them popping up, it may be because a tree was pruned too severely. Using hand pruners or loppers, cut the sucker at its base, as close to the tree as possible. If you catch the suckers early, when they're small, you may be able to pull them up with your hands. Always do this as soon as you see the suckers. Don't wait; they grow fast and stress your tree.

Water sprouts are much like suckers, since they are weak growths that do nothing for the tree. Water sprouts, however, appear growing straight upright on tree branches. (See illustration, page 64.) Cut these off because they interfere with the tree's healthy growth.

Raising the canopy of a tree—a name for removing the lower limbs up to 10 or 12 feet—is an easy and rewarding pruning job for the homeowner. This is usually considered part of training a young tree because it's better to remove small limbs than large ones because larger pruning wounds take longer to heal. But if you have a deciduous tree in your yard that blocks people from walking beneath it and blocks light from reaching the grass or plants beneath the tree, you'll want to remove the lower limbs gradually over 3 or 4 years. (Remember the rule: Never remove more than one-fourth of a tree's growth at any one time or in any year.) Don't be too eager to start this process if your tree is newly planted. Wait until it's been in your yard 3 or 4 years. Those small

When branches cross, they rub against each other and often rub the bark off. This gives damaging diseases and insects a place to enter the tree.

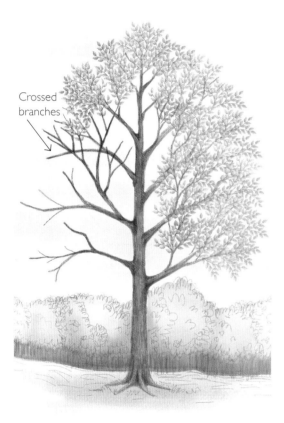

Crossed branches

Suckers

Tree roots can send out suckers, which, if not removed, will grow into new trees. Pull up all suckers when they appear.

(Left) Water sprouts appear on tree limbs or trunks. These weak shoots interfere with the growth and appearance of the tree and should be removed promptly. (Right) A tree with a double trunk is weak and may eventually split. Prune a young tree so that it has only one central leader, or trunk.

Water sprouts

Double trunk

WHEN TO HIRE AN EXPERT

Some tree pruning is simple and easy, but other tasks—especially when pruning is required because of disease, insect infestation, or storm damage—may be more safely accomplished by a professional, called an arborist. These experts are experienced and insured, which gives you peace of mind. But many people like the challenge of DIY and think they'll save money by taking care of needed tree pruning on their own. So, how do you know when it may be best to call a professional? Here are 10 situations in which you should consider handing over the job to an expert arborist.

1. You will be working very close to power lines, next to a busy street or road, or simply over fences, structures, cars, and other trees or desirable shrubs that might be damaged by unexpectedly falling tree limbs.

2. The tree has been damaged by a storm, insects, or disease. It's not easy for a homeowner to know simply by looking what portions of the tree are weakened by decay and need special attention.

3. When a tree has fallen or partially fallen in a storm, pinning a car or structure beneath. Often, the heavy weight of a mature tree in this situation calls for professional attention. Be especially careful when the ground is covered with snow or is rain-soaked.

4. You don't have another person to help. Pruning trees is never a solitary job. Two or three people on the ground, serving as lookouts—carefully watching all aspects of the job—make it safer for you and your surroundings.

5. The branches to be removed are very heavy or large.

6. The area needing attention is near the top of a tall tree, or it's difficult to reach.

7. The area in which you would be working, in the tree and below it, is in tight quarters.

8. The work is over your head (unless you're standing on the ground and using a pole saw).

9. You aren't comfortable with heights or don't feel safe standing halfway up a tall ladder, holding onto the ladder with one hand and the other holding and using a sharp saw.

10. You don't have the necessary equipment, or don't want to buy it for one-time use.

branches on the lower portion of the trunk do help the tree by preventing sunscald of the bark, and their leaves increase photosynthesis, helping the tree grow better.

Look at how the limbs are attached to the trunk of a tree. The best angle is wide—forming a 45-degree to 60-degree angle. A more upright connection, or crotch—in a V shape—is weak and likely to break off under stress such as wind or snow. Remove the limbs that have V-shaped crotches, preferably when the tree is young. If the tree is more mature, use the three-step technique of removing a mature tree branch (see page 66).

Don't let a tree develop two or more trunks because a tree with two trunks growing together is in danger of splitting part at some point in its life. Remove any competing central leaders that try to develop. When the tree is mature, do this over a period of 3 years.

The Best Times to Prune Deciduous Trees

It's easy to know the right time to prune most flowering or shade trees in your yard. With flowering trees such as dogwoods and saucer magnolias, wait until blooming is over (the exceptions to the rule, below, are pruned in winter). Winter is the ideal time to prune just about all non-flowering deciduous trees. (See page 26 for a list of trees that should *not* be pruned in winter because they "bleed" sap unless they are pruned in warm weather.) Without leaves or flowers in the way, you can more easily see what needs to be pruned on a tree and how and where to make your cuts. When pruned in winter, trees will often recover faster because they're primed to begin growing when spring arrives.

DON'T PRUNE THESE FLOWERING TREES RIGHT AFTER BLOOMING

Most deciduous trees that produce prominent flowers are pruned right after their blooms fade. But the trees below prefer to be pruned in winter, or shortly afterward. Those that like to be pruned in late winter or early spring shouldn't be pruned in the coldest part of the year because low temperatures may damage the pruned tree.

Crape myrtle, late winter or early spring

Franklinia, winter

Golden raintree, winter

Linden, late winter or early spring

Mimosa (silk tree), late winter in warm-winter climates and after last spring frost in cold climates

Royal poinciana, late winter

Sourwood, winter

Stewartia, winter

Tree of Heaven, winter

Tulip poplar, winter

How to Remove a Large Tree Limb

1-2-3. That's all it takes to safely remove a large limb from a deciduous tree. If you try to just cut off a branch in one step, it can injure whatever's or whomever's beneath the tree. It also can tear off some of the trunk's bark, which can allow insects or diseases to enter. As shown below, start about 6 to 12 inches out from the trunk *and from the underside of the branch,* and use a pruning saw to cut one-fourth to one-third of the way into the branch. Then move 1 to 3 inches beyond the first cut and farther from the trunk. Cut the branch all the through from the top until it falls to the ground. Then go back and carefully cut away (from the top) the remainder of the branch, being sure not to make a cut that's flush with the trunk but just outside the branch collar (see the photos, page 62). The branch collar contains a natural chemical that protects the tree from decay and speeds healing.

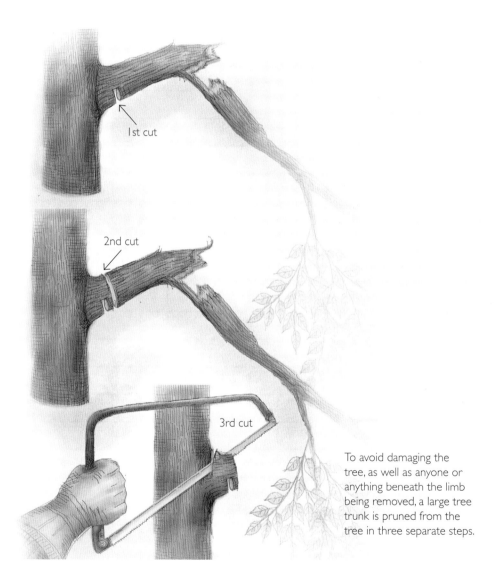

1st cut

2nd cut

3rd cut

To avoid damaging the tree, as well as anyone or anything beneath the limb being removed, a large tree trunk is pruned from the tree in three separate steps.

How to Train a Young Tree

You've heard the biblical advice, "Train up a child in the way he should go and when he is old, he will not depart from it." That adage also applies to trees. If you'd like your trees to be handsome, healthy, and rarely needing pruning attention, start by regular pruning for a purpose when the tree is young. What sort of purposes? Your goal will be to encourage only one trunk per tree; to promote strong, evenly spaced scaffold branches that are the main framework for the tree develop; and to correct weak crotches (where a branch connects to the trunk at a narrow, not wide, angle, causing the limb to break under stress such as plenty of snow, strong winds, and so forth).

Right after you've planted your young tree, laterally prune (page 18) any broken

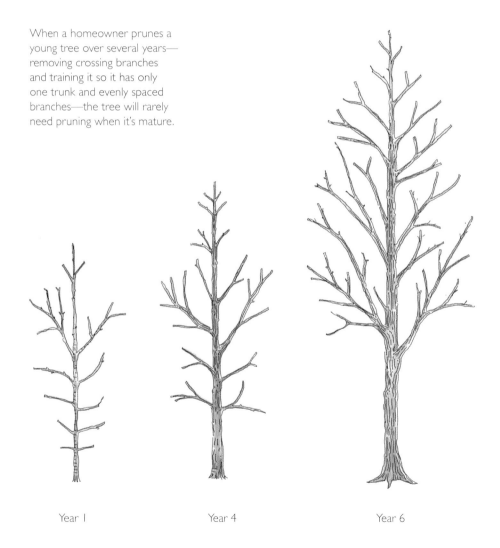

When a homeowner prunes a young tree over several years—removing crossing branches and training it so it has only one trunk and evenly spaced branches—the tree will rarely need pruning when it's mature.

Year 1   Year 4   Year 6

or damaged branches to about one-fourth an inch above a healthy bud. Don't do any more pruning in the first year unless it's to remove damaged limbs; leave the tree alone to concentrate on its most important task for the next couple of years—developing a good root system.

When the tree is 3 or 4 years old:

• Begin removing the lower branches. Cut them back to the trunk, without leaving a stub or cutting into the branch collar. (See page 62.) Do this over 4 or 5 years, eventually having the lowest limbs start about 10 feet up in the air.

• If more than one trunk, or central leader, tries to develop, cut it out. With the exception of Japanese maples, crape myrtles, and a few others, you want trees with only one trunk.

• Next, look at the main branches, or scaffolds, that grow from the trunk. You want to consider their size, the angle at which they grow, and how far they're spaced from other branches. Keep branches that are smaller in diameter than the tree's trunk or that aren't so long they stick out much farther than the other limbs (although you never want all limbs to be cut to the same length). The best angles for the branches to connect to the tree are 45 to 60 degrees. Smaller than that and the growth dies at the point where the two join. Scaffold limbs typically are kept about 18 inches apart. That helps give the tree balance. Be careful as you select branches to remove; you eventually want limbs evenly spaced all around the tree, not just on one or two sides.

• Use thinning cuts to remove branches as necessary. If it becomes necessary to shorten a branch, even temporarily, use a lateral cut (page 18) that's made just above a healthy bud.

• Keep in mind that this is a several-year project, and you shouldn't remove more than one-fourth of the tree's growth whenever you prune.

How to Prevent "Crape Murder"

In the South, crape myrtles—trees and shrubs, depending on the eventual size—are the most incorrectly pruned plants. Unknowing homeowners generally prune back the plant's upward-growing branches to stubs, often at the same place year after year. One of the problems is that these stubs

With proper pruning a crape myrtle can be a lovely plant.

or knots aren't attractive during winter when the tree or shrub is bare. It also prevents the trunks from developing the nice mottled bark that they're known for. And, most important, this type of pruning creates weak new growth for the next year, which allows the flowers to flop over and lessens the plant's summer appearance (which is when you want it to look great). "Crape murder," the term for this commonly seen mispruning, has been popularized by Steve Bender of *Southern Living* magazine. He even maintains an annual online Crape Murder contest to discover the ugliest pruned crape myrtle across the South and Texas.

Here's how to prune a crape myrtle correctly.

First, decide on your goal. Most crape myrtles need to be thinned out so sunlight can penetrate into the interior. You may also want to space the trunks evenly for the same reason and to show off the exfoliating (peeling) bark.

You'll need a sharp pair of hand pruners for removing twiggy growth, loppers for stems that are about ¾ to 1½ inches in diameter, and a pruning saw for branches larger than that. If you are working on a really tall crape myrtle, pole pruners can be useful.

In late winter or very early spring, begin pruning by removing any suckers at the base of the tree. Then remove any damaged or dead branches by pruning them back to the trunk. Thin all side branches that are growing from the bottom 3 or 4 feet of the trunks. Cut them back to the trunk, not leaving any stubs. Look for branches that are crossing or rubbing and remove one of each pair. Now you should thin out branches that are growing toward the interior of the tree. Don't overdo it the first year. Stick with the rule of removing only one-fourth of the branches. You can do more next year. But at the end of your session you'll have a more graceful, attractive crape myrtle, and when summer arrives, you'll find that it continues to look good and it blooms better too. And no one was guilty of crape murder.

But if you're trying to correct a previous "murder," cut below the knots in winter. When growth begins in spring, a number of new stems will appear in the cut area. Prune off all but one new stem and let it grow. Do this again the next couple of years until the knots are no longer visible.

Just as homeowners often don't know how to prune a crape myrtle to bring out its beauty, they frequently don't understand how to prune an evergreen tree, so backyard evergreens are left unpruned and grow much too large. But that, too, is a problem with a solution. Read on.

CHAPTER 7

How to Prune Evergreen Trees, from Hollies and Magnolias to Firs and Pines

Evergreen trees, as you know just from their name, are those that stay green all year. But there's more than one type. Some, such as pine and spruce, have needles. Others, such as holly and southern magnolia trees, have thick leaves and are referred to as broadleaf evergreens. There are a couple of important differences in pruning evergreens that don't apply to deciduous trees (more on those in a minute). But mostly you'll prune these trees using the same techniques that you've already encountered. The good news is that evergreen trees require little pruning except to correct damaged, diseased, or dead branches. Unfortunately, it's hard to greatly reduce the size of a mature evergreen (see page 72). That's the reason it's important to choose a tree that won't grow too large for your yard and to lightly and regularly thin (see page 20) the tree when it's young, to keep it the needed size.

The Big Difference About Pruning Evergreen Trees

The most important thing you can remember about pruning evergreen trees—especially needled evergreens—is *never* to cut into the branches at a point where there are no needles or leaves. Unfortunately, no new growth will develop from these inactive areas of evergreen trees because they have few if any active lateral buds (page 16) and you end up with a visible dead stub because there's nothing to conceal the cuts you made. To prevent the problem, make pruning cuts only into live or green wood (which is producing needles), *not* back into old, bare wood. This devoid growth area is the main reason that it's extremely difficult to renovate an overgrown needled evergreen tree.

Do not prune so far back on the limb of an evergreen tree that there are no green needles, since no new growth will sprout from that spot.

Another Difference: Pinching to Make Pine, Fir, and Spruce Trees Bushier

Nice thick growth is desirable on evergreens, and one easy way to develop it in fir, pine, and spruce trees is to pinch back the *candles* (the new growth at the ends of stems) that appear in late spring or early summer. That's when the new needles are in a tight cluster but have not become hard. They'll be about 2 inches long. With your thumb and index finger, pinch off one-third to one-half of each candle and dispose of them. Don't use pruners, loppers, or shears because that will cause the needles that remain to become brown.

Pinch off one-third or one-half of a pine tree's candle, or new growth. That causes bushier growth.

Shearing Needled Evergreens

It's okay, but not necessary to lightly shear needled evergreens with power hedge shears in order to help the tree develop and maintain its natural shape. Some professionals advise against it, but many people like the look that results, if it's done well. The main thing to keep in mind is to shear off only a small amount of growth; if you get back into sections of branches that aren't growing, the appearance of the sheared tree will be worse, not better. Trees that are often sheared because they respond well to it are Deodar cedar and Lawson cypress.

Don't shear evergreens—or prune them at all—during droughts. You want all a tree's energy to go toward survival, not recovering from pruning that could have been postponed. Also, new growth, often

encouraged by pruning, will be difficult if the tree is water-stressed.

While the best shearing results come from using power shears when the ground and tree are a little damp, *never* use electric shears under these conditions. Instead, switch to a gas-powered hedge trimmer. Manual hedge shears don't do as good a job on evergreen trees as they do on frequently sheared hedges; you'll be happier with the appearance of evergreen trees sheared by power equipment.

Although it's possible to shear some broadleaf evergreens, such as holly, the tree's leaves will be cut in half and the resulting shape is more likely to be artificial than natural, so should you stick with thinning rather than shearing broadleaf trees, although, yes, it takes somewhat longer.

A tree's *central leader* is its main trunk (which, on needled evergreens, you'll be dealing with mostly at its top portion, near the terminal bud; see page 16). Evergreen trees have strong central leaders. If one begins to develop a second trunk, remove it. If a leader gets broken near the top of a needled evergreen tree, it's important to help the tree replace it so it doesn't grow several competing central leaders, which can weaken the tree and destroy its natural form.

If that happens, here's what to do: Bend upward a small, young branch just below the damaged central leader and attach it to the damaged central leader, or if there isn't much of it left, to a stake you've tied to the tree's trunk. Leave it in place until the new leader is growing upright on its own accord (1 to 2 years), then remove the tie and stake.

Broken
central leader

Repaired
central leader

If a needled evergreen tree's central leader gets broken, choose a strong branch from just below the broken leader and gently bend it so it's facing upward, rather than sideways. Then tie it to a stake that's been attached to the trunk. Within a couple of years, the new branch will become the tree's central leader.

Keep These Tips in Mind

The two main goals to keep in mind for pruning all kinds of evergreen trees are:

• Maintain a strong central leader and trunk.

• Encourage and maintain the natural form or shape.

Thinning (page 20) is the best technique for pruning every evergreen tree, broadleaf and needled. (The only exception is palms; see page 77 for more about palm trees.) Thinning enables the tree to maintain its natural shape and always look normal by removing dead or broken branches and trimming growth that's out of bounds. Typically, light annual pruning of evergreens is better than waiting

TIMING

Remove one-third or one-half of candles on pines and similar needled evergreens in late spring or early summer. Most other pruning on broadleaf and needled evergreens can be done almost any time during the year *except* late summer and fall. These are the best times:

Late Winter
• Arborvitae (major pruning; do light pruning in early summer)
• Chaste tree (in mild climates; spring for cold climates)
• Juniper
• Spruce (but pinch candles in late spring or early summer)

Early Spring (before new growth begins)
• Cedar (except Deodar cedar)
• Cherry laurel
• Douglas fir (prune in late spring to control size)
• False cypress (*Chamaecyparis*)
• Fir (but pinch candles in later spring or early summer)
• Holly (major pruning; light pruning anytime)
• Plum yew
• Southern magnolia
• Sweet bay magnolia

Late Winter or Early Spring (before growth begins)
• Bay tree (major pruning; light pruning in spring or early summer)

• Bottle tree
• California live oak
• Camphor tree (major pruning; do regular pruning anytime)
• Japanese cedar (major pruning; do regular pruning in spring or summer)
• Strawberry tree
• Yew (light trimming can be done anytime)

Other Times
• China fir, spring and summer
• Cypress, late spring and summer
• Deodar cedar, late spring
• Hemlock, spring or summer
• Olive tree, anytime
• Palms, anytime
• Pine, pinch candles in late spring or early summer
• Podocarpus, anytime
• Red-flowering gum, after flowering
• Redwood (including giant redwood), anytime
• Southern live oak, early winter

and doing a bigger job every 3 or 5 years. To thin an evergreen tree, remove a branch back to the trunk so it leaves no stub. This method opens up the tree a bit for light to penetrate the interior, which is good for it. However, if it becomes necessary to remove a large branch from any kind of evergreen tree, do it using the three-step process explained in the chapter on pruning deciduous trees. Be very careful not to make the final cut flush with the trunk but just outside the bark collar (page 62).

How to Overcome Negligence or Poor Pruning

When you move to a new house, sometimes you find that evergreens have been pruned incorrectly or allowed to get out of shape. Many times, these mistakes can be corrected, but a big dose of patience will be required since evergreens usually grow more slowly than deciduous trees. So you'll need to take your time rather than hurrying and risking further damage.

1.   Make sure the plant has a central leader. Correct the situation if there's more than one central leader at the top of tree. (See page 74.)

2.   Then go back and read (page 20) about thinning and begin light thinning at the proper season. Never remove more than one-fifth of the branches. (Fewer is better in the beginning.) Do this each year for 4 or 5 years.

3.   Try to redevelop the tree's natural shape gradually by pruning out sections that interfere with the normal shape. Any "holes" that have resulted from poor pruning may take several years to grow back together.

Don't Remove Lower Limbs

Because the lower limbs of deciduous shade trees are typically removed at least 10 feet above the ground, many homeowners continue this practice with needled and broad-leaf evergreens, possibly because that makes it easier to mow around the tree. But for aesthetic reasons, it's better to leave the lower limbs on evergreen trees, which tend to lose their natural shape and look top-heavy if their leaf or needle growth starts many feet in the air. When lower branches are removed, rarely does the tree replace them with new branches so the look is permanent. Another advantage of keeping limbs that grow all the way to the ground is that they may hide some of the debris generated by evergreen leaves (old leaves from southern magnolias, for example, and cones from pines). This keeps your yard looking neater.

Because of their height and stately beauty, evergreen trees add a sense of permanence to a yard. They are going to be part of the landscape for a long time, so it makes sense to take the best possible care of them and to begin pruning these trees gently when they're young so they're grow up to be all that you hope for.

How to Prune Palms

Palm pruning is mostly maintenance—removing faded flower clusters, dead leaves, leaf bases, and brown fronds such as those seen below. These mar the attractive appearance of the tree and are a fire hazard. All can be removed at their base anytime during the year that they have dried. Since palms are generally quite tall, you might want to consider whether it isn't better to hire a professional instead of doing it yourself. One job that a homeowner can readily perform is digging out suckers from beneath date palm trees. For young trees, train palms to a single trunk.

CHAPTER 8

How to Prune Roses

Do you hesitate to prune your roses back each year? Maybe you think that the more of the bush you cut off, the fewer flowers will appear. Or you wonder where and when to prune. Or you hesitate because those bushes are, after all, covered with sharp thorns and you'd rather not get your hands and arms scratched up. Actually, pruning is good for roses. It shortens canes, which causes more new growth, and that, in turn, produces more flowers, everyone's main reason for growing roses. Pruning also can help keep rosebushes healthy, avoiding diseases such as blackspot and mildew. And to escape scratches, you'll want to find a pair of the long gloves made especially to wear when you're pruning roses. These protect both hands and arms and are essential, you'll find, if you own more than a couple of rosebushes. Those who love roses and want to grow more of them soon learn how to improve them through pruning.

General Rules for Pruning Roses

Your goal in pruning roses is simple: to encourage new growth (that's where new roses come from) and to make sure the center portion of the bush isn't so crowded with canes and leaves that little light and air reach the interior. Plenty of sunlight and good air circulation are keys to preventing the fungus diseases that can be so prevalent on roses.

Although specific types of roses—hybrid teas, climbing roses, Knock Out—have individual requirements for pruning (see pages 84–89), these overall directions apply to all roses.

• Before you plant a new rose, look it over to see if any of the canes or roots (on a bare-root rose) are dead or damaged. If so, clip them back.

• Wait until a rose is at least 1 year old before you prune it, except to remove dead or damaged canes.

• Unless you're cutting canes back to the ground, always make any cuts just above a bud that faces the outside of the bush. (See page 83.) That encourages and directs new growth.

It's easy to tell if you've cut into dead or live wood on the canes when you're pruning. Live wood looks white or very light tan when it's cut. Dead wood is brownish. When you cut into a brown portion of a cane, make another cut farther down to find live wood. That will lead to new growth.

When doing your main spring pruning on any rose except a miniature, remove all canes that are thinner than a pencil.

Remove suckers promptly. In spring or summer, dig down into the soil and pull up any suckers that appear at the base of your rosebush. Cutting them off seems to encourage more growth, so twisting them off or pulling them up is recommended. Wear thick gloves and remove all of the sucker's root as well as the top. While you may think suckers are harmless and will provide you with more of the desirable roses you love, they won't. They sap nutrients from your bush and are generally such vigorous growers that they take over. For information about removing suckers that are growing below the bud union on the bush itself, see "Why Does My White Rosebush Have Red Flowers?" on page 89.

Before planting a bare-root rose, trim off damaged or dead roots.

Heavy versus Light Pruning

Experienced rosarians may differ in the amount they prune from a bush in spring.

Heavy or hard pruning is the practice of leaving only three to five canes on the bush and cutting those back to about 6 inches high. It's used mostly for renovating a neglected bush, although it can produce fewer but larger flowers than usual, making it useful for those competing in rose shows. Heavy pruning also generates more regrowth but is harder on the bush.

Moderate pruning is the most-used method. It involves leaving all canes except those smaller than a pencil in diameter and pruning them back to about half their height.

Light pruning means leaving all healthy canes on the bush but cutting back about 20 percent of each. It results in more roses than heavy pruning does and they will bloom sooner, but the roses will be smaller and often not as well-shaped.

A rose-pruning method you may not have heard of is called "easy," and it is. Using gas- or electric-powered hedge shears, cut the canes of a mature or overgrown rose in half, straight across the bush. Then remove any dead or damaged canes with loppers or hand pruners. It sounds weird, but it works, according to the American Rose Society.

When a rosebush is heavily pruned (left), it will produce fewer but larger flowers. Light pruning (right) removes about 20 percent of the bush and results in smaller flowers that bloom sooner.

Rose Pruning Timetable

Early spring, before new growth starts, is the main time to prune roses that bloom over and over during the summer. Most rose growers know it's time when the bright yellow flowers of forsythia appear in their region (this can be from January until April, depending on the part of the country).

Summer is the time to prune heirloom roses and climbers that bloom only once a year (generally in or near June, depending on the climate). Do needed pruning soon after flowers fade. For other types of roses, do light pruning as you cut off individual roses to take them indoors for arrangements or as you deadhead faded flowers. Cut the stem to either the first or second cluster of five leaves on the stem below the flower. Cutting back to the first cluster is good on hybrid teas and bushes that are weak, while many rosarians prefer to cut to the second cluster on floribunda roses and any others that produce clusters of flowers, rather than single blooms and on vigorously growing bushes. Deadheading this way enables the bush to produce more flowers, saves plant energy that would otherwise be devoted to trying to produce seeds from the old flowers, and even opens the bush up more to air circulation.

In fall, cut to ground level any long, thin canes that could be whipped around by boisterous winds, which can loosen the bush's roots. Also remove rubbing or crossing canes, which can cause damage. But because of the threat of injury from cold weather, don't do any other rose pruning in fall; wait until after the worst of winter is over.

When to *Stop* Pruning

Homeowners like to prune in fall because the weather is moderate and they have less to do in the yard than in spring and summer. But to avoid injury from cold weather, it's important that you stop pruning about 6 weeks before your area's first hard frost. (If you don't know when that is, call your county's extension service office and ask.) For instance, you may want to leave rose hips, left, the decorative fruit developed from the faded flowers, on the bush over winter, removing them in spring. If you do, the birds will thank you, as they're very fond of them.

Don't remove the last roses of the season and you may be surprised that the old blooms become rose hips, bright red or orange seed pods, which are attractive in the late fall garden and liked by birds.

The Right Cut

When you're pruning a rose—even deadheading spent blooms—make your cuts at a 45-degree angle about ¼ inch above a cluster of five leaves or above a bud that's facing the outside of the bush. The cut should slant away from the bud, not toward it. If you cut straight across the cane, water can stand on the end and cause rot. With an angle, the moisture rolls off. Because you've cut near a bud, which will become a terminal bud (page 16), that's where new growth is directed. Generally you want that new growth to head toward the outer portion of the bush so the center doesn't become overcrowded and lacks light and good air circulation, both of which are necessary for a healthy rose.

To prevent rose borers from drilling into the cut ends of pruned canes, it's best to seal the ends of the canes right after you finish pruning, using white glue or orange shellac.

To prevent damage from borers, seal the ends of just-pruned rose canes with white glue or shellac.

Prune rose canes at the 45-degree angle (left) and slightly above a bud that faces the outside of the bush.

How and When to Prune Different Types of Roses

Climbers and Ramblers

The main question about pruning climbing and rambling roses is the right time to do it. The answer depends on how often the rose blooms during the season. If it flowers repeatedly, it receives its main pruning in early spring, when forsythia blooms, just as most other roses do. But if it blooms only once a year, it's pruned as soon as flowering finishes. If you're not sure, wait and prune after blooming; then, if roses appear later in the summer, remember to prune your climber the next time in early spring.

Climbers and ramblers should cover a certain area. That's why we plant them where we do: along a rail fence, next to an arbor or a trellis. If we cut them back to 2 feet tall each year, they would never have the long canes that earn them the name "climbers." So generally they're pruned lightly. You also don't start pruning them—except to deadhead faded flowers and to remove winter damage and dead canes—until they've been in your yard about 3 years. Not only does this preserve the long canes you want and need, but it encourages lateral growth off these canes, and that's where the roses will appear.

Start by removing dead or diseased canes and all winter damage. Then prune out (back to a main branch) any crossing branches. On older ramblers and climbers that may not be blooming as prolifically as before, remove one or two of the non-blooming canes to ground level with loppers or a pruning saw. If the rose is growing out of bounds, shorten the lateral canes back to ¼ inch above an outward-facing bud, so that it fits its support. For severely overgrown plants, you may cut the canes back short enough that they contain only three buds per cane. (Some rose growers prune all lateral canes of established climbers and ramblers back to five buds yearly.) Look at the bud union (that knobby round knot near the base of the plant) and remove all suckers or canes that are growing from *beneath* the bud union. Seal the ends of the cut canes with white glue or orange shellac. Then tie the climber or rambler to its support. It will bloom better if grown more horizontally than vertically.

David Austin Old English Roses

David Austin recommends both summer and early spring pruning for its shrub roses, which can become too big otherwise, especially in warm climates.

In early spring, cut back Old English roses from David Austin by one-third to one-half, keeping a rounded shape to the bush. In summer, cut off faded roses. Reprune any extra-tall canes back to the same height as all the others.

Rambler roses and climbers usually are pruned lightly. If they bloom only once a year, prune right after they flower instead of in late winter, as with most other roses.

Wait to prune Old English shrub roses until they're more than 1 year old. Then cut them back by about one-half in early spring, maintaining a rounded shape. For a larger shrub, cut it back by one-third. For a smaller one, remove two-thirds of the length of the canes. Remove all dead or damaged canes. Seal the ends of the cuts.

In summer, instead of regular deadheading Old English shrub roses, David Austin advises that you cut each flowering stem back to two or three sets of leaves. This encourages repeat flowering and helps shape the shrub rose. If one cane grows much higher than the others, don't cut it down completely. Instead, trim it back to just above a cluster of five leaves so that the cane is the height of the other canes.

For established Old English climbers and ramblers, cut horizontal canes back to three or four sets of leaves in summer. In early spring, remove dead, diseased, damaged, or weak canes. Ramblers may need less pruning; just remove old canes as necessary.

Floribundas, Grandifloras, and Polyanthas

Floribunda roses form smaller, shrubby bushes and bear roses in clusters. 'Europeana' and 'Betty Boop' are among the most popular floribundas. Polyanthas, such as 'The Fairy', are the forerunners of floribundas and are pruned like them. Grandifloras combine characteristics of floribundas and hybrid teas. Grandifloras are tall, with larger, elegantly shaped flowers borne in clusters. 'Queen Elizabeth' is one of the best known grandifloras.

Because floribundas and polyanthas are often grown in groups or as small hedges and their smaller flowers are considered a garden display rather than cut for bringing indoors, they're generally pruned fairly casually, rather than precisely, which could take too long. In early spring, use loppers to remove dead or damaged canes, crossing canes, suckers (see next page), and weak growth. Leave thin canes in place. Then cut the bush back by one-fourth (one-third

Watch for signs of winter damage on Floribundas in early spring, and cut away dead canes.

Begin pruning a hybrid tea rose by removing all dead and damaged canes, as well as those that are smaller than a pencil in diameter.

for an older bush that's too large). It should ideally be at least 18 inches tall after pruning. Seal the ends of the cuts after you finish to deter borers.

Grandifloras are pruned like hybrid teas.

Hybrid Tea Roses

In early spring, remove dead or damaged canes as well as suckers that have grown up from the soil and those that have appeared from beneath the bud union. Remove twiggy growth that's smaller in diameter than a pencil. Cut canes back to half their original height, cutting to above an outward-facing bud. Or you may remove, at ground level, all but five canes and cut those back, above

buds, to about 1 foot high (24 inches for a grandiflora). Seal the ends of the cut canes with orange shellac or white glue.

Knock Out and Other Reblooming Shrub or Landscape Roses

These popular shrub-type or landscape roses (which may be more like groundcovers) are very easy to care for, and that includes pruning. As with other roses, you remove any dead or diseased sections when you notice them. Then you prune in early spring to control the shape and size. Beginning the second year the rose is in your yard, cut the canes back to about 2 feet high, making the cuts at a slant above

The oh-so-popular Knock Out roses triple in height after spring pruning, so if you want a bush that's 3 feet high, prune it back to 1 foot tall in early spring.

a healthy bud. If the plant is seriously overgrown, you may cut the canes back to 1 foot high. Remove some of the canes in the center of the bush to open it up to more sunlight and better air circulation. Prune away crossing branches. Seal the ends of cut canes to prevent damage from cane borers. Deadheading is usually not necessary, as the blooms are likely to fall off by themselves after they fade.

Miniatures

In early spring, cut back all growth by one-third. Then remove canes so that five to eight of the thickest canes are left. Don't worry about suckers because miniature roses aren't grafted. But do remove any dead or damaged canes. That's it for pruning until after blooming. When flowers are fading, remove them with sharp scissors or hand pruners and shape the small bush to a rounded shape, slightly taller in the middle. Don't worry too much about cutting to just above a bud. It's nice if you can, but tedious and not really necessary. Indoors, you prune mini roses just the same.

A rosebush will look better and bloom more prolifically if it's pruned each year.

Old Garden Roses

These old-fashioned beauties are pruned lightly. When depends on whether they flower once during the season (prune after flowers fade) or are repeat bloomers (prune in early spring).

Tree Roses

Also called standards, tree roses have leaves and flowers atop a tall, bare cane. They often grow in containers, but may be planted in the ground, mostly in mild climates. In hot climates, you'll need to protect the cane from sun damage by placing the stake on the side the sun comes from. During the growing season, pinch off any growth that appears on or at the base of the long cane. In early spring, remove damaged, dying, or rubbing canes and weak growth. Then cut back the top growth by half. If some canes are growing out of bounds and changing the shape of the standard, prune them back to above a bud. As you deadhead during the summer, try to make your cuts to maintain the top's symmetry

Pruning a rose gives you more flowers and a handsome bush in the garden. The only thing that might enhance this beauty is to have a charming vine (purple clematis, anyone?) trained up a pillar nearby. Vines are not hard to prune, as you'll find in the next chapter.

Q: WHY DOES MY WHITE ROSEBUSH HAVE RED FLOWERS THIS YEAR?

A: It's because many rosebushes are grafted onto rootstock of another type of rose, which is very vigorous and therefore helps the top of the bush to grow faster and more energetically. They're joined at the bud union (the swollen growth on the trunk) near the base of the plant. Usually the rootstock produces red flowers. That doesn't generally affect the top flowers unless you don't prune off all growth that sprouts from beneath the bud union, because that growth will be from the rootstock. In order to restore your bush to the original color, take your hand pruners and cut off all the stems that lead back to beneath the bud union, and be vigilant about removing any others that try to sprout from that area. Don't be tempted to leave the canes that are producing the red flowers, thinking that it's interesting to have both colors on one bush. If you do, the red will quickly predominate and you'll no longer have any white, pink, or yellow flowers at all.

CHAPTER 9

How to Prune Clematis and Other Vines

A young, flowering vine is so attractive in a yard. It, and a legion of other vines, can brighten a mailbox, hide a chain-link fence, produce flowers and fragrance, block the sun, hide an eyesore—all while planted in a small square of earth. But in only a few years, that neat little vine may become a tangled mess instead of a desirable landscape feature. The reason is simple: many vines are overly aggressive growers and shouldn't be planted on typical urban or suburban properties. But even mild-mannered vines, such as clematis and Carolina jessamine, can grow into a tangle because few homeowners know how to prune a vine—or have the courage to tackle it. Actually, though, pruning a vine isn't any more complicated than pruning a shrub, and it is done much the same way. You already know how to do prune shrubs, so vines will be simple.

What, When, and How

Pruning a vine starts with knowing what you want to accomplish. It might be controlling size or shape, encouraging more flowering, removing weak stems, or directing new growth onto a support. That will determine how you prune and, occasionally, when.

Vines that bloom on *new wood* (stems that grow the current year) are cut back in early spring before the plant starts growing. Prune vines that bloom on *old wood* (which is the previous season's growth) are pruned after they've finished flowering. Total renovation of a vine is usually done in late winter, to encourage vigorous new growth beginning in spring.

How to Prune Vines

At planting time: Shaping a vine properly begins when you plant it—and cut it back about half at the same time. Yes, that's hard to talk yourself into doing. After all, you want to see your new vine grow and flower quickly. But cutting back the vine to

---

WHEN TO PRUNE VINES

Late Winter
- Cardinal vine
- Dutchman's pipe
- Five-leaf akebia (in warm climates)
- Moonflower
- Porcelain vine

Early Spring
- Beach pea (in cold climates)
- Boston ivy
- Bittersweet
- Creeping fig
- Crossvine
- English ivy
- Silver lace vine
- Star jasmine
- Stauntonia
- Sweet pea (in cold climates)
- Sweet potato vine
- Virginia creeper
- Wire plant

Late Winter or Early Spring
- Allamanda
- Climbing hydrangea
- Hops
- Kolomikta vine (*Actinidia*)
- Mandevilla (non-hybrids)

- Scarlet kadsura
- Trumpet creeper
- Wintercreeper

After Flowering
- Beach pea (in warm climates)
- Bougainvillea
- Five-leaf akebia (in cold climates)
- Honeysuckle (gold flame and trumpet)
- Mandevilla (hybrids)
- Sweet pea (in warm climates)
- Showy jasmine
- Winter jasmine

Other Times
A few vines are pruned outside the regular times. They include:
- Allamanda (late spring or early summer; pinching)
- Clematis (see page 94)
- Coral vine (late fall or early winter)
- Passionflower (spring)
- Trumpet vine (winter and several times during summer)
- Wisteria (winter and spring; prune in summer to reduce the growth rate)

no more than two stems and three strong side shoots really encourages new growth. Make your cuts at a 45-degree angle about ¼ inch above an outward-facing bud.

Regular pruning: Prune mature vines by occasional pinching in the summer to keep the vine in shape, by removing dead or damaged portions when they appear, and by using heading back (see page 18) to encourage branching and thinning (page 20) to remove congested growth.

Overgrown vines: Prune in late winter or early spring, before new growth begins. If possible, remove the vine from any support and lay it on the ground so it will be easier to work with. Cut off the old excess growth and dispose of it. Just as you did at planting time, leave two young stems at the bottom of the vine and three healthy side shoots on each. Remove all the others. That may seem like too much, but you'll be amazed at how much new growth takes off after spring arrives. Of course, from now on, it will be better to keep up with regular pruning, so you don't end up with another messy vine.

Vines that are bare at the bottom: Cut back to 3 or 4 inches tall and let regrow. You may need to assess if the bottom of the vine is receiving enough sun.

Aggressive vines: It's best, of course, to avoid these vines altogether. Or, if you have one, to remove it from your yard because they spread so much, so quickly, and require a lot of work on the homeowner's part. But if you want to keep your wisteria, Japanese honeysuckle, and so forth, you'll need to be diligent about pruning the vines in winter (when you leave three or four buds on each stem) and again right after flowering (when you cut the current year's growth back to

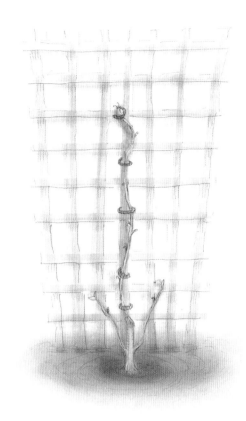

A young vine gets off to speedy growth when pruned and then tied to its support.

about a foot long). That preserves flowering and helps keep overly aggressive growth in check. If you don't mind missing one year's blossoms, you can thin the vine in late winter or early spring.

It's reassuring to find out that pruning vines is really quite easy—and when done regularly, can make a huge difference in the plants' appearance. In the next chapter, you'll discover some ways—possibly new to you—to shape fruit trees to ensure that you get much larger crops of apples, peaches, pears, and other favorites. Just like pruning vines and rosebushes, once you've pruned fruit trees for the first time, these techniques will seem simple to you too.

When it comes to growing, blooming, and pruning, all clematis vines are not the same. Usually they're divided into three groups according to when they flower and if they produce those flowers on new wood, old wood, or both. If you know the name of your clematis vine, you can look up its pruning requirements online. Or you can observe when and how the blossoms appear and follow these directions. Be sure to dispose of all trimmings as yard waste.

Group A: These clematis vines flower in spring on stems that grew the previous year. These vines don't usually need much pruning to keep them in shape, but if you need to head back (page 18) a few stems to encourage more branching or thin (page 20) back to a bud to keep the vine in bounds, do it lightly and right after flowering. These clematis vines don't respond well to being cut back to ground level. (Clematis in Group A include all that bloom only in spring, such as *C. armandii*, *C. occidentalis*, and 'Fragrant Spring'.)

Group B: These are large-flowered clematis that bloom in early summer on stems that grew the previous year and generally rebloom lightly later in the season on new growth. In late winter or early spring, prune away all dead, damaged, or weak wood. Then cut back the tips of the stems (ending above a bud) after the second flowering has finished. (This group includes all double-flowered clematis, 'Nellie Moser', and 'Belle of Woking'.)

Group C: This is the easiest collection of clematis to prune since they flower late in summer on stems that grew that year. In late winter or early spring, before new growth appears, simply cut the vine back to about a foot high, making sure that each stem has two buds on it. (Clematis in this category include Jackmanii hybrids and *Clematis viticella as well as sweet autumn clematis.*)

Sweet autumn clematis is a loved but very aggressive vine that's trimmed back to about 12 inches tall in late winter or early spring.

CHAPTER 10

How to Prune Fruits and Nuts

What a treat to be able to eat fresh apples, peaches, blueberries, or grapes that you've picked in your own backyard. But anyone who's ever seen an abandoned orchard or blackberries that have taken over a field realizes that a bountiful fruit harvest on a healthy plant depends upon regular pruning. Various fruits grow in different ways—blueberries as shrubs, grapes on vines, pecans and peaches on trees—and are consequently pruned by diverse methods. It's important to learn and follow the various techniques for pruning the fruits you have, and not just because they produce much more fruit that way. Proper fruit pruning also increases the quality and size of the fruit you harvest, can help decrease insects and diseases, increases plant longevity, and aids in preventing damage to the plant. Most fruit growers recognize that those benefits are worth devoting a little time to pruning every year.

Why and When to Prune a Fruit Tree

There are three main ways to train and prune fruit trees that will create strong limbs that won't break in storms or when bearing a heavy load of fruit: the central leader method; the modified central leader method; and the vase, or open-center, method. Each method also lets in plenty of sunlight, increases air circulation, decreases tree size where necessary, and makes it easier to pick ripe fruit. If you need to remind yourself about what the technical terms in this section mean and how and why to perform heading and other techniques, go back to pages 17 to 21.

Timing is important in pruning fruit trees. You need to do dormant-season pruning after the worst of winter's cold has passed to avoid damage to the tree. (Your local Extension service office will be able to give you the best pruning dates for your location.) Prune apple and pecan trees first, then do cherry, peach, and plum trees. Always prune older trees before younger ones.

Techniques for Pruning and Training Fruit and Nut Trees
Central Leader Method

A tree trained to a central leader form (used mostly for apples, pears, pecans, and plums) has a single main trunk (called the central leader) and groupings of three or four scaffold branches—horizontal branches that are evenly spaced around the trunk—starting about 36 inches above the ground. The lower branches will be the longest, and the length of each group of branches above that will be slightly shorter, like a pyramid. This lets in as much sunlight as possible. Trees that are left unpruned and develop several trunks, rather than a central leader, often break when the tree develops a big crop of fruit. Fruit trees trained to a central leader also develop faster and produce larger crops.

First Year

Spring, after Planting

A young fruit or nut tree is often bought as a straight stick (called a whip) with no branches. After planting, wait until early spring when you see the new buds ready to burst into growth. Then head back the tree (that is, cut it from the top; see pages 18) so that it's about 24 to 30 inches tall for a dwarf tree;—30 to 36 inches for a tree that will be full sized. This will encourage branches to form.

If you bought a fruit tree growing in a container or one that has branches already on it, leave three or four branches, starting about 24 to 36 inches above the ground. You want branches that are evenly spaced—about 12 to 18 inches apart vertically for regular trees, 6 to 12 inches for dwarfs—and growing in different directions. Head these young scaffold branches back by about one-fourth, then remove the others. Always cut any dead or damaged branches back to live wood.

Summer

If any branches are growing upright and are challenging the main trunk as a central leader, cut them off. To make sure that the scaffold, or main, branches grow from the trunk at wide angles, use a clothespin or small piece of wood to hold the limb at a 60-degree angle

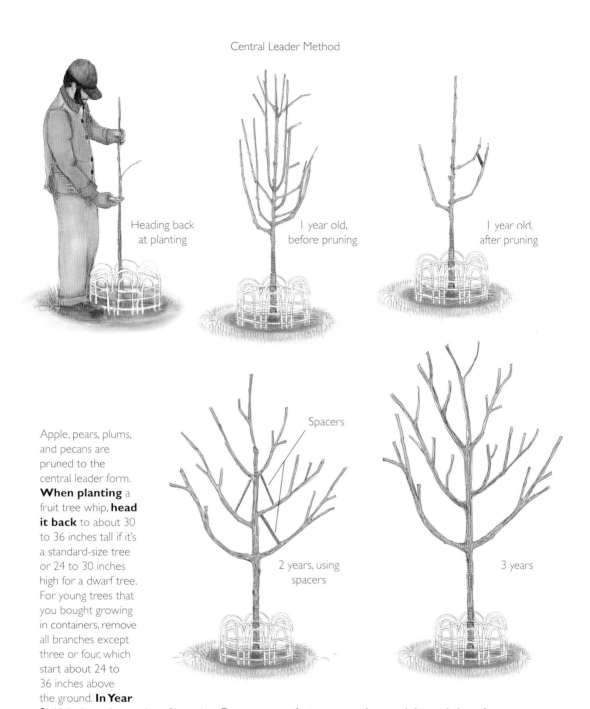

Central Leader Method

Heading back
at planting

1 year old,
before pruning

1 year old,
after pruning

Spacers

2 years, using
spacers

3 years

Apple, pears, plums, and pecans are pruned to the central leader form. **When planting** a fruit tree whip, **head it back** to about 30 to 36 inches tall if it's a standard-size tree or 24 to 30 inches high for a dwarf tree. For young trees that you bought growing in containers, remove all branches except three or four, which start about 24 to 36 inches above the ground. **In Year 2**, think about the spacing of branches. **Remove any that are growing upright and therefore challenging the main trunk.** Branches that are attached to the trunk at a narrow angle are weak; those attached at a wide angle are stronger. Use spacers or spreaders to encourage fruit tree limbs to grow at 60-degree angles to the trunk. These can be wooden clothespins, commercially available spreaders or pieces of wood left from pruning. Gently place them between the branches. **At the end of the second year**, choose three or four new limbs evenly spaced about 6 to 12 inches apart for dwarf trees and 12 to 18 inches apart for standard trees. Remove all others, as well as suckers and water sprouts. In Year 3, do the same things you did in Year 2, including selecting three new branches. Now your tree is trained to the central leader form and will be probably begin producing fruit soon.

from the trunk. Leave it there until the branch grows at the correct angle on its own. It's okay to leave small shoots as temporary growth that grows from the trunk and develops foliage to help protect the trunk from sun damage. Head them back to 12 inches long and remove them permanently at the end of the third year.

Late Winter

If you started with a whip, late in the first winter is the time to select the first scaffold branches. Just as was done with container-grown trees earlier, choose three or four branches that are about 12 to 18 inches apart vertically for regular trees or 6 to 12 inches for dwarfs and growing from the trunk in different directions. Head them back (see page 18) about one-fourth to encourage them to develop secondary branches. Also head back the new growth on the central leader to about 12 to 18 inches above the highest scaffold branch.

Second Year

Just as you did the previous year, remove any vertical growth that's trying to become a central leader. (You can do this in winter or early spring.) In late winter, again choose three or four scaffold branches above the first tier of branches and remove back to the trunk or central leader those that aren't needed. Head back all scaffold braches by one-fourth and also head back about one-third of the new growth on the vertical leader. Remove any growth that's crossing or rubbing.

In summer, remove any suckers at the base of the tree and any water sprouts (vertical growth, see page 62) on branches. Often, water sprouts develop on limbs that have been spread to wider than a 60-degree angle. If so, narrow the angle. You may also need to insert more wood or clothespins as spreaders on the new scaffold branches.

Third Year

In late winter, select the third and last grouping of three evenly spaced scaffold branches and remove any others that are growing from the trunk (including the foot-long temporary shoots that you allowed to remain on the trunk). Head back one-fourth to one-third of the new growth on the central leader and one-fourth of the growth on the older scaffold branches.

In summer, use spreaders to develop wide crotch angles on the branches as necessary. If fruit develops on the central leader or the youngest scaffold branches, remove it because it will cause them to bend.

Fourth Year

Remove water sprouts and suckers in summer. Continue to spread young branches that need it to a 60-degree angle from the trunk. Pick off fruit that develops on the central leader and young branches. In later winter, maintain the tree's pyramidal shape by shortening braches that are growing out of bounds. Remove new branches that try to grow from the central leader. Or if additional limbs have been allowed to develop, remove them over the next 2 to 3 years. Keep one central leader, or trunk, and remove any competing vertical growth that tries to become a second central leader. Remove any rubbing or crossing growth. By the end of the fourth year, your tree will be trained in the way it should grow and be ready to start producing a good crop of fruit, if hasn't already.

Modified Central Leader Method

Apricots, persimmons, sweet and sour cherries, and walnuts may be pruned to a modified central leader form, which combines the central leader shape and the vase shape (page 102). Apples may be pruned this way too. The modified central leader method produces a tree that's open to plenty of sunlight, which results in lots of fruit.

Start by pruning your tree using the directions under the central leader method. Do this for a tree's first 3 years in your yard. In late winter of the fourth year, when the tree is approximately 6 feet tall and has six to eight well-spaced scaffold branches, head back (page 18) the central leader, or main trunk, to just above the highest branch. At the same time, cut all the scaffold branches to an outward-facing bud. From then on, follow the directions for the vase, or open-center, method.

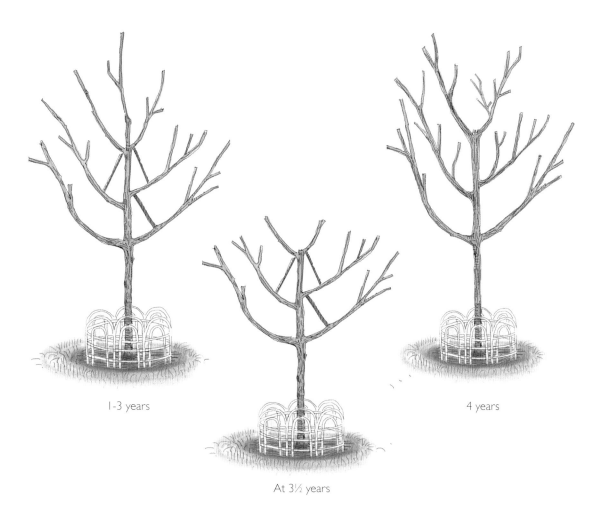

1-3 years

At 3½ years

4 years

The modified central leader form follows the central leader method for the first three years and then it follows the directions for the vase, or open center, method.

Vase, or Open-Center, Method

The vase method creates a tree with a short trunk and three or four wide scaffold branches. It's used for peaches, nectarines, Japanese plums, crab apples, almonds, and, occasionally, for sour cherries. It introduces good sunlight into the center and other parts of the tree, eliminating shade, which can be a problem in fast-growing species.

During Late Winter

After planting a whip, or unbranched fruit tree, cut the whip of a dwarf tree back to ¼ inch above a bud that's 2 feet above ground level. For a standard-sized tree, cut the whip back to above a bud that's 30 inches from the ground. On young trees that already have branches, leave three or four that are evenly spaced around the trunk, not directly opposite another branch, and about 22 to 28 inches above the soil. (That's so you'll have room to work beneath the tree.) If none meet that criteria, cut them off. If you were able to retain scaffold branches, cut them back to where each has three buds. Preferably the end bud will be facing the outside of the tree.

Summer

Select three or four branches uniformly spaced around the trunk, if this wasn't done during the winter, and remove all other branches that appear. Begin to train the scaffold branches with pieces of wood or clothespins so that they develop wide crotch angles. (See page 66.) Also remove any water sprouts or suckers.

Next Three Winters

The next three winters, head back (page 18) the scaffold branches about one-third to an

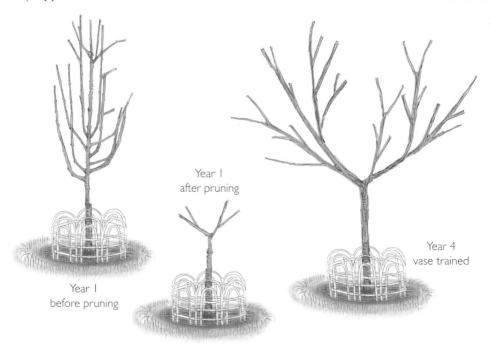

Year 1
before pruning

Year 1
after pruning

Year 4
vase trained

The vase, or open center, method of pruning fruit trees is used especially for peaches, nectarines, Japanese plums, and almonds. It allows plenty of sunlight into the center of the tree.

outward-growing bud in order to encourage branches and to build strength. Remove any upright growth that appears in the center of the tree or on the trunk. You don't want excess shading, which causes fruit growth only on the ends of branches. That will break the branches if the fruit load becomes too heavy. Anytime that you prune, always remove dead, damaged, or diseased wood as well as shriveled fruit left from the previous season. If it ever becomes necessary to remove a large branch from the tree, follow the directions for pruning mature deciduous trees (page 66).

Tips for Pruning Specific Types of Fruit Trees

Apples

Train to the central leader form. Learn to recognize spurs (below), which are stubby branches less than 6 inches long that grow flowers and later fruit. These live a long time, so be sure not to remove or damage them when pruning or picking fruit. Continue to maintain the central leader, or trunk; don't let more than one develop. Also prune in

Fruit spur

Protect fruit spurs from damage since these are what produce flowers and then fruit.

later winter to maintain the pyramid or Christmas tree form that's required.

Apricots

Train to the modified central leader form. Unlike apples, the spurs on which apricots are produced last only 3 or 4 years and so are removed more regularly. Regularly thin the excess growth on an apricot tree in late winter to encourage more fruit production. In years when frosts kill the flowers or fruits, prune lightly. In some climates, apricot growers prefer to wait until after flowering to prune.

Cherries, Sweet and Sour

Train according to the modified central leader method or, for sour cherries that you'd like to keep smaller, the vase shape. Don't let young trees grow too tall or harvesting will be difficult. To avoid that, in midsummer, remove tall upright growth at the top of the tree trained to a modified central leader shape and thin (page 20) several of the lowest branches. Do other pruning, such as annually thinning weak growth and heading back all new shoots by one-third, in late winter. If the limbs of young sweet cherry trees grow 6 feet long without developing branches, head them back by one-fourth to encourage branching. Wide crotch angles are essential on sour cherry trees because the limbs of these trees are more brittle and prone to break. Cherries bear on 2-year-old spurs; you'll want to remove unproductive spurs and other wood that doesn't bear fruit.

Citrus

Citrus trees, typically trained to a central leader or modified central leader form, need little pruning beyond regularly removing water sprouts, suckers, and damaged wood. Thinning the interior of the tree to allow more light and air circulation often helps prevent insect problems. Cutting back lower branches so they don't touch the ground also discourages insects. When a tree is injured by cold, wait until early summer to cut branches back to new wood. Don't be concerned that the early form isn't what you may be used to: growth often begins as upright shoots, which will eventually develop side branches. Don't remove more than 20 percent of the foliage at any time, because the trunk and limbs of citrus trees are easily scalded by the sun.

Figs

Depending on the climate, figs are generally grown as trees or bushes. As trees, train figs into the vase, or open-center, shape. Keep the branches from touching the ground and remove suckers. Cut winter-damaged wood back to live wood after the weather has warmed reliably. Figs usually bear one crop a year in late spring on old wood. (It may sometimes be eliminated by winter cold.) Then figs bear a second crop later in the season on new wood. Be aware when you're pruning that you may be removing either of these crops.

Peaches and Nectarines

Prune to a vase, or open-center. form. When grown in a marginal climate, wait until early spring to prune. Because they produce fruit on wood that grew the previous year, annual pruning is needed to keep new branches and more fruit coming along. Water sprouts often appear and should be removed regularly during the growing season. Prune from ladders, rather than climbing in the trees, to avoid damaging the bark.

Pears

Train to a modified central leader with four or five main scaffold branches. Remove water sprouts regularly but otherwise prune lightly to avoid undesirable growth. Watch out for fireblight (brown leaves with a scalded appearance) and remove diseased portions of branches, cutting back about 1 foot into new wood. When dealing with diseased wood, always disinfect your pruners by dipping them in full-strength Lysol between each cut.

Persimmons

Prune young Japanese or Oriental persimmons to a modified central leader with three scaffold braches that you've trained to have wide crotch angles. If you have a native persimmon in your yard, it will grow fine in its natural shape, with little pruning required except to control its size, if needed. Thinning will increase the size of Japanese persimmons, but not the fruit on native trees.

Plums

The two main types of plums are European and Japanese. Prune European plums to a central leader and Japanese plums to a vase, or open-center, form. Thin European plums lightly to maintain the tree's shape. Japanese plums tend to grow and bear assertively and so need more frequent pruning, starting after their fifth year. Thin out

When tree fruits grow too close together, thinning (removing some of the fruits so the others are farther apart) causes the fruits that remain to grow larger.

about one-third of new growth each year in late winter. Head back long, thin branches by one-fourth to one-third.

How Thinning Fruit Produces More Fruit

It's one of the hardest things the owner of a young fruit tree is ever asked to do. After he has planted, pruned, and tended that tree for 3 or more years, when the first fruits finally appear to great cheers, he's told to remove some of them. Surely that couldn't be right! But here are several good reasons to bite the bullet and actually pick off some of the fruit:

• The remaining fruit will be larger and of better quality.

• A slightly smaller crop avoids the danger of breaking a tree limb.

• A too-large crop can weaken the tree.

• It can help prevent the spread of disease.

GUIDELINES ON HOW FAR APART TO THIN FRUITS

Apples, thin to one fruit per cluster or, for heavy crops, 6 inches apart

Apricots, 3 to 5 inches

Citrus, 2 to 6 inches

Peaches and nectarines, 4 to 6 inches

Pears, thin to one fruit per cluster, or 4 to 6 inches between fruits

Plums, 3 inches

• When fruit isn't thinned, trees often do what's called "alternate-year bearing". One year they produce little fruit and the next year, an exceptionally big harvest. It's better for the tree, as well as the harvester, to have a constant crop each year.

Some trees naturally drop part of their fruit each year, usually from May to July (it's called the June drop, although the actual timing depends on where you live). This is natural thinning. Fruits that generally don't need to be thinned include cherries, citrus, figs, and persimmons, although you can thin them if needed. You also don't have to thin nut trees routinely.

It's important to thin fruit early in the season, when apples and pears reach about ½ inch in diameter and stone fruits have grown to ¾ inch. Always remove diseased or damaged fruit and any that are much smaller than all the others. Generally you do this by hand, except in very tall trees where a pole pruner is more practical.

How to Renovate an Overgrown Fruit Tree

A fruit tree that hasn't been pruned in years isn't likely to bear much desirable fruit. The good news, though, is that most can be brought back to healthy, bearing condition if pruned patiently over a period of 3 years.

Year 1: In late winter or early spring—after the worst of winter is over but before the tree has generated any new growth—thin away all dead, diseased, or damaged portions of branches. Prune off branches

An old, overgrown fruit tree should be renovated over a period of several years so it will once again bear good fruit.

An old, neglected apple tree certainly looks different after it has been pruned. Don't worry; within 3 years, it should be productive again.

that grow downward or grow straight up. Thin out thick clusters of branches that prevent light from getting to the interior of the tree. Remove any crossing or rubbing branches. Starting at the top of the tree, remove one-third of excess limbs.

Year 2: In summer, remove water sprouts and suckers. In later winter or early spring, repeat Year 1's pruning activity. Also remove branches that are weak or too small and new growth that has become crowded.

Year 3: Repeat Year 2, pruning to maintain the form that the tree is trained to and keeping only the number of scaffold braches that are called for, pruning away the new growth that isn't needed. If you need to remove large branches, follow the instructions on page 66.

How to Prune Nut Trees

Nut trees usually grow quite tall and do double duty in the yard—they produce shade and delicious nuts to eat. Pruning will enhance the shape of the tree and increase nut production.

Almonds

After planting almond whips, cut them back to 36 inches tall. During the next several dormant seasons, train each to a single leader. After the young tree has been trained, prune lightly as needed to keep lower limbs at least 3 feet off the ground and thin to keep the center of the tree open to allow in light. Always remove dead, damaged, or diseased branches. Regular pruning of mature trees tends to decrease almond yields, some studies have shown, so it isn't recommended.

Black Walnuts

Prune by the central leader technique. The trees often try to produce multiple leaders. In late winter, remove branches that try to compete with the single leader.

Chestnuts

Train to the modified central leader system. Staking is often needed to get the central leader off to a strong start. The first winter, choose two scaffold branches, spacing them evenly. The next winter, thin to an outward-facing bud any branches growing toward the trunk of the tree. This encourages a wider tree. In the third or fourth winter, head back the central leader. In subsequent winters, thin out crowded branches in the center of the tree.

Filberts/Hazelnuts

In late winter after planting, prune back the young tree to 30 to 36 inches tall. Also head back all side shoots by one-third. Choose three to five scaffold branches for the tree and remove all others. In summer, remove all suckers growing from below the area where the tree was grafted. When the tree is mature, thin some of the top branches to let in light.

Macadamias

Train to the central leader system. The tree wants to develop multiple trunks, so remove competing leaders as they appear. You may need to lightly stake the single trunk for a year. After the trunk has grown 5 feet tall, allow evenly spaced side branches to develop. Instead of allowing the branches to grow opposite each other on the central leader or trunk, space them about 6 inches apart on alternating sides of the trunk. Pinch back tips of the new branches every other winter to induce more branching. Spread crotch branches with scrap wood or clothespins to develop wide crotch angles that won't break.

Pecans

Train by the central leader or modified central leader method. After planting, head back the whip to 36 to 40 inches tall. The first winter head back the central leader by one-third. Remove the next strongest shoot back to the trunk. Pinch off the tip of the third-strongest shoot and also any small shoots that develop below the larger shoots. The second winter, cut back about one-third of the central leader's new growth. Again, remove the second-strongest shoot near the central leader and pinch 2 inches from the tips of all side shoots. In the third through fifth winters, do the same as in the second year, but also remove side branches, starting at the bottom of the tree and working up, when they become about 1 inch in diameter. Also, tip prune side branches. Let the tree develop 6 to 10 scaffold braches evenly spaced 8 to 14 inches apart around the central leader.

Walnuts

Train to a modified central leader system. To avoid winter damage, wait until early spring to prune. Head back the central leader when it reaches 8 to 9 feet tall and remove any shoots that are competing with it. The second and third seasons, select scaffold branches evenly spaced around the trunk about 8 to 12 inches apart vertically. The branches shouldn't be directly opposite one another on the trunk but alternating. Avoid branches with narrow crotch angles, which easily break under pressure. Branches that are attached to the trunk at wider than 45-degree angles, on the other hand, won't grow well. Remove branches that compete with the scaffolds.

Techniques for Pruning Blackberries, Blueberries, and Shrub-Type Fruit

If you don't have room in your landscape for a fruit or nut tree, fruits that grow on shrubs can be an excellent solution. Blueberries need so little pruning and special attention that they're a wonderful deciduous shrub for yard use whether you want the fruit or not. And anyone who's ever sighed over the price of a half pint of fresh raspberries at the supermarket is delighted to learn how little it costs to grow them at home—and their pruning is very straightforward.

How to Prune Brambles

Although not all have actual thorns, blackberries, boysenberries, and raspberries are called brambles or, sometimes, caneberries. They don't form a neat bush, as blueberries do, so it helps to understand how they grow. The roots are perennial, so they last a long time. But the canes of most brambles are biennial, which means they come up and grow one year but don't produce fruit until the second year. After they fruit, the second-year canes die, so you'll want to cut them back to the ground, leaving first-year canes to grow and produce fruit the next year. As with all other fruits, remove dead, diseased, or damaged canes at any time.

Blackberries

It's vital to prune blackberries each year or they'll get out of control. In midsummer, pinch or cut the tips of all first-year canes on erect-growing blackberries so they're about 4 feet tall. When pruned at this height, they won't need to be trellised. In winter, pinch or tip prune all lateral or side shoots on first-year canes so they're about 12 to 14 inches long. The next year, after the fruiting season is over, cut back to the ground all canes that bore fruit and dispose of the clippings away from the garden. Also remove suckers and other growth that pops up where you don't want it. Once you have a mature blackberry, space canes to about 6 inches apart in winter to avoid overcrowding.

When blackberries become too crowded (left), they won't bear fruit abundantly or be as easy to pick as once they've been pruned to a more manageable size (right).

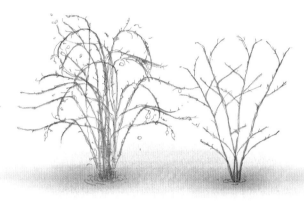

Boysenberries

These are pruned like blackberries, but the canes are usually pruned to no more than 8 feet long and tied to a trellis.

Boysenberries are pruned as blackberries are, but are tied to a trellis, which makes picking easier.

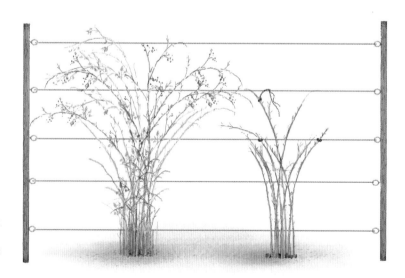

Raspberries

Several types of raspberries are popular, each of which is pruned in slightly different ways.

• *Summer-fruiting red and golden raspberries*—In early spring, remove all dead, diseased, or damaged canes and cut all canes to 4½ feet high. As the plant matures and produces excess growth, thin canes to about 5 inches apart in early spring. After fruiting, cut all canes that fruited to ground level.

• *Black and purple raspberries*—In early spring, thin lateral branches back to 8 inches long. In early summer, as the plants reach 24 to 30 inches tall, remove the end 3 inches from each cane tip. After harvest, remove the canes that bore fruit.

• *Everbearing raspberries*—These produce fruit in spring and again in fall. They are the exception to the rule that bramble canes die after fruiting since their canes fruit twice before dying. To have two crops a year, cut the tips of the canes back 3 inches in fall after harvest. After the next spring or summer harvest, cut the canes that fruit back to the ground. In late winter or early spring, thin excess canes until they stand 5 or 6 inches apart. If you want everbearers to produce one large crop of raspberries instead of two smaller ones, cut all canes back to the ground in early spring.

Don't let raspberries get too crowded or production will plummet.

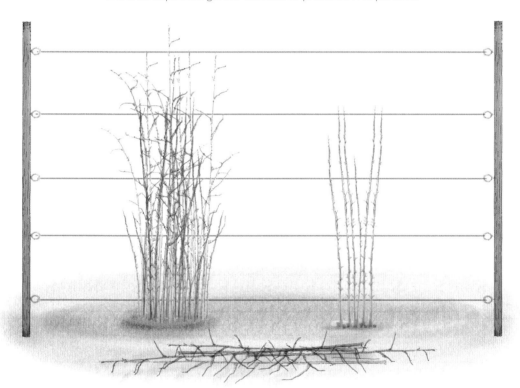

How to Prune Shrub Fruit

Fruit bushes need occasional thinning to let more sunlight into the center of the plant.

• Blueberries—Little or no pruning is required until the bushes are 5 or more years old. In the early years, annually remove canes that are crossing or rubbing or have become diseased or damaged. In the second and third years, rub off the flower buds so the bush will direct its growth to canes and leaves, not fruit.

Once the bush is 7 years old, begin removing one or two of the oldest and largest canes each year in early spring, since these will be the least productive. To rejuvenate a neglected blueberry bush, you may cut out up to 20 percent of the oldest growth in early spring for 3 years. Blueberry bushes should grow upright but have growth that's open enough to allow light inside.

• Gooseberries—In the late winter or early spring after the plant's first year of growth, remove those branches that grow

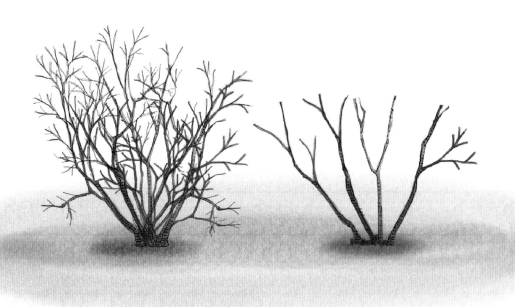

Blueberries usually need little pruning, but to renovate an overgrown or neglected bush, prune out one-third of the cane each year for 3 years.

along the ground and all canes except for eight vigorous canes, which are left to grow. In the second winter, prune away excess canes, leaving four canes from the first year and five canes that grew over the previous season. In the third year, leave three or four canes from the first, second, and third growing seasons. The fourth and following winters, remove back to ground level the oldest canes and leave three canes each from the previous growing season. This removes old, unproductive wood and ensures that new, productive wood is always growing to take its place. The fruit grows on 1-year-old wood and also on spurs on 2- or 3-year-old wood.

How to Prune Fruiting Vines

Grapes and other vining fruits can be more complicated to deal with than shrubs or trees because they must be trained to a specific trellis system and pruned back in a particular way. But once you've grasped the techniques, you'll be fine. If grapevines are ignored, they'll become an unfruitful mess.

Beginning the second year that gooseberries are in your yard, all but eight or so canes are pruned to ground level. In following years unproductive canes are pruned away.

Grapes

There are several ways to train grapes and therefore more than one way to prune them. However, it's important to remember that in all methods, you'll get the most grapes from 1-year-old canes. If there are no 1-year-old canes (because you cut the entire vine back), you won't get much fruit. The same is true if you didn't prune at all and all the canes are old ones.

Grapes are grown one of four main methods—four-arm Kniffen system, cane pruning, spur pruning, and on an arbor—and each method is pruned differently.

Four-Arm Kniffen system—After planting, cut off all shoots but one and head it back so that it has three buds. When new growth is about 1 foot long, select a vigorous upright shoot and head it back so it has four buds. Remove all other shoots. Tie the chosen shoot lightly to a stake, and all summer continue attaching it to the stake so it grows uprightly. When it grows as tall as the bottom wire, head it back so that it will branch. Allow two branches to grow, each on opposite sides of the main shoot or trunk, and tie them so they grow along the horizontal wire. Allow the other shoot to continue growing up. When it finally reaches the top wire, pinch out the top 3 inches of the stem. The next winter, remove all growth except the main trunk and two more side branches at the wire above the first side branches. Head back the side branches so they are shorter, containing

Cane pruning is the method for American and French-American types of grapes because they produce fruits farther along the canes than European grapes do.

about 10 buds each. The following summer, remove all shoots that appear on the trunk. The fourth year, it's time to choose whether to continue with a cane or spur system. The Extension service office in your locality will be able to tell you which will be best for the type of grape you're growing.

Spur system—For best success with grapes grown according to the spur method, prune them hard each winter. Remove any shoots appearing on the trunk and also weak growth on the lateral or side vines. You want to remove all shoots except 1-year-old canes, which will produce fruit. The best 1-year-old canes will be thicker than a pencil and close to the trunk. Prune so that you end up with the shoots (spurs) spaced about 10 inches apart along the horizontal

arm, with each spur containing two buds. From those buds will grow two shoots that will produce fruit the next summer. The next winter after fruiting, remove any growth from the trunk, cut back diseased, damaged, or weak growth. Cut spurs with 1-year-old wood back to two buds. Remove old spurs that have fruited.

Cane system—In the fourth and following winters, remove to the trunk all wood that bore fruit the previous year. Look for canes that grew the previous year (lighter brown wood) and select one on each side of the trunk near each of the horizontal wires and train them to the wires. Do the same thing with four new canes, which will be renewal canes, producing spurs that will yield fruit in 2 years. Prune

The four-arm Kniffen system is one of the most common ways to train grapes. It appears much like a two-wire fence, but you can see the four "arms" of the grape vine growing on it.

the renewal canes back to two buds on each. Prune the fruiting canes so they have 8 to 10 buds on each. Prune the same way in future years.

Sturdy arbor—Grow one vine up each post, removing all but the strongest cane and tying it to the post as it grows. The first winter or early spring, head back the vine so it will produce side branches. (If you don't do this, but just let the vines grow on their own, they'll produce plenty of leaves for shade but not as much fruit.) In following years, remove vines that fruited, cut back the previous season's growth to six buds, and head back four or five canes from the year before so they have three buds. You want to have productive canes spaced about 2 to 3 feet apart on the trellis so that they'll cover the arbor in summer but won't be a tangled mess.

Muscadines

Muscadines (also known as scuppernongs) are a native American grape grown in warm climates. The fruits are large and have a thick skin. It's much easier to prune muscadines when they're young than if they've been allowed to grow out of control. Prune in early spring before new growth appears or the cut portions of the vine will "bleed" sap. This isn't harmful but attracts insects and doesn't look good.

As with grapes, you want to train a muscadine to one trunk. Off of the trunk, allow four cordons, arms, or horizontal canes to grow that are trained along trellis wires. Because the fruit is produced on last year's growth, which is lighter brown than older wood, you'll need to cut back all of the previous year's wood so that three or four buds

Grapes grown on the spur system are pruned back hard each winter.

are left on the previous season's growth. In the beginning you'll be tempted to leave more than four buds, figuring that will produce more fruit. True, it does, but too many buds also cause lower-quality fruit. In early spring, always remove dead or damaged wood and tendrils that wrap around the cordons or arms. That's it—every year in early spring, cut back last year's growth to three or four buds and remove tendrils so they don't girdle the cordon.

Kiwis and Hardy Kiwis

Kiwi and hardy kiwi are fast-growing vines that are usually trained to a T-bar trellis or support. Female and male plants—you need one of each (or one male to eight females, if you're growing a lot)—are pruned differently. Prune kiwis when they're completely dormant because if they are pruned too late, sap bleeding occurs.

When planting kiwis, cut back the main stem to 1 foot tall (so it has one or two buds) and train it straight up the trellis stake, tying it lightly as it grows. The first winter, remove any other shoots that have grown. Remove suckers at the base of the plant when you see them.

The second winter, head back the trunk when it reaches the top of the trellis. Choose two buds on opposite sides of the trunk and train them perpendicular along the center wire of the trellis to form arms or cordons. Head these two cordons back to wood that's ¼ inch in diameter or slightly larger.

The next winter, tie the cordons to the wire about every 2 feet. Leave new growth that appears on the cordons about every foot and tie it to the outside wire of the trellis. In summer, prune off all other shoots and suckers.

In the winter of the third growing season, cut the cordons and new shoots back to wood that's larger in diameter than a pencil. Continue attaching the cordons to the wire and the shoots left last winter so they grow perpendicular to the cordons.

Remove any frost damage on kiwis when it occurs (females are more prone to winter injury than males, while kiwis grown on their own roots are hardier than grafted plants). Wind damage can also be a problem and should be removed quickly.

Pruning established female kiwis: In late winter, remove canes that fruited and about 70 percent of the last season's growth. Leave new canes that grew at the base of the canes that fruited last season; remove any tangled growth. Aim for a 15-foot mature vine that has 30 or more buds spaced evenly on both sides of the vine.

Pruning established male kiwis: The purpose of the male is to produce flowers to pollinate the female vines, so all pruning is aimed at creating lots of flowers. Prune lightly in winter, just enough to keep the vine from getting tangled and messy. After flowering, prune male vines as you did female vines in the dormant season.

Hardy kiwis: Although hardy and regular kiwis are generally pruned and trained the same, the cordons or side arms of hardy kiwis may need to be replaced each 3 to 4 years. In winter, cut them back to above a bud on the main trunk.

While pruning fruits can seem complicated at first, the next chapter's discussion of grooming annuals, perennials, and houseplants will show you the other side of pruning—simple actions that can make a big difference.

CHAPTER 11

Grooming Annuals, Perennials, Herbs, Vegetables, and Houseplants

Grooming is a low-key type of pruning that can make a noticeable difference. The annual flowers in your yard—marigolds and zinnias, for example—will bloom more prolifically and longer, if you remove old flowers as soon as they fade. (That's called deadheading.) Keep an annual geranium plant in compact shape and blooming bountifully by pinching back the tips of its stems in spring and early summer. Or encourage impressive dahlia or rose blooms by removing (disbudding) one of two or three flower buds that grow next to each other; the bud that remains will produce a much larger flower. Herbs will taste better if you pinch off the first and second flush of flowers that develop on the plants. That's because herb leaves and stems—the desirable parts—have a stronger aroma and taste if they're harvested before the plant blooms. It seems counterintuitive that removing part of a plant can make it bloom and look better—but it's true. Try it and see for yourself.

Houseplants

The initial reason to groom a houseplant is to remove a dead or dying stem or leaf. You've no doubt done that before. For the health of the plant, use a sharp pair of scissors or hand pruners if the stem is too thick to pinch off. (If you have a lot of houseplants, you can find small, lightweight pruners that do this job easily and quickly.) Make your cuts or pinches close to a stem.

You'll also want to deadhead a flowering indoor plant. Just pinch off the dying blossoms and toss them out.

Some houseplants grow too vigorously and need to be trimmed back so they'll fit in the location where they've been placed. To reduce the size, wait until the plant has started growing in spring and use hand pruners to gently cut back stems (up to one-fourth their length; no more at one time) to just above a healthy bud.

To shape a houseplant that needs minor correction to its size or shape, just pinch back (with your fingers) the top inch of each stem.

Annuals

Many annual flowers need deadheading to keep them in flower from spring until fall, and sometimes the gardener needs to pinch or cut them back slightly so they don't get leggy (produce weak, tall growth) but grow into a compact shape. Pinching back the tips of stems often causes the

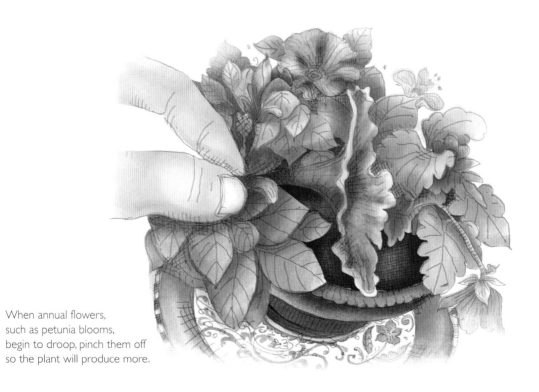

When annual flowers, such as petunia blooms, begin to droop, pinch them off so the plant will produce more.

Remove faded daylily flowers to prevent the plant from producing seeds. Seedpods lessen desired plant and flower growth and look messy.

plant to bloom more prolifically too. Use hand pruners on thick stems, such as those of geraniums. Don't do this until the plant is at least 5 inches tall, and make sure it's actively growing.

On annuals such as coleus, which can develop insignificant flowers that signal a coming decline in the stems and foliage, gardeners use their fingers to pinch out the tiny flowers as soon as they appear in order to keep the foliage in tip-top shape as long as possible.

Perennials

Deadhead perennial plants so they'll look better in the garden. Deadheading will often cause some perennials to rebloom. Snap off the seedpods that pop up at the top of daylily stalks unless you want the seeds inside these to mature and ripen so they can be planted to produce other daylilies (not like the ones from the plant that produced the pods, though). When a perennial needs pinching back to improve its size or appearance, do it lightly—with your hands, remove just the tips of the stems. The exceptions would be cutting back by half perennials that flowered in spring to improve their appearance as summer-flowering perennials begin their show. It also encourages new growth on the spring-flowering plants. When groups of perennials have become somewhat crowded (but not quite enough to dig them up and replant), thin the plants by removing about one-third of the stems (back to the ground). This is especially helpful for perennials that might develop mildew since it opens up the plants to more air and sunlight. Cut weather-beaten summer-flowering perennials back by one-third after they've flowered to keep the garden looking neat. You may delay the time that chrysanthemums flower by cutting off flower buds soon after they appear. If the gardener pinches off all the developing flower buds until about the middle of July, the plant will bloom, as expected, in fall when few perennials are putting on a show. But if the flower buds are left on the plant, the mum will bloom in summer, when so many other plants are also in flower. Experienced gardeners also experiment with cutting back other perennials by a few inches in late spring or early summer to delay the plants' flowering until later in the summer.

Herbs and Vegetables

We've already mentioned the importance of delaying herbs' blooming by pinching out developing flowers so that the harvest will be more flavorful and fragrant. If you regularly harvest your herbs, no more pruning may be needed. That will usually keep the plants in good shape. But woody perennial herbs, which come back year after year, can become floppy if they're not trimmed back at least annually (in spring, just after new growth has appeared). Using hand pruners, trim stems back by one-fourth to one-third. Make your cut slightly above a pair of leaves. Perennial herbs can get too crowded and need to be thinned just as perennials are.

Just about any vegetable from squash to tomatoes can be pruned—if needed—to remove diseased or insect-damaged portions and encourage greater growth and more abundant fruits and keep a plant from getting out of bounds. Pinching off some excess leaves will help a tomato plant stay inside its cage or support. So will removing those little suckers that appear between a stem and a branch. Yes, those may grow and produce tomatoes, eventually, but they greatly increase the size and weight of a tomato plant, often making it too big for an ordinary home garden. It's easy to pinch them out as you see them. (If you want to, you can root these to form new plants.) Near the end of the growing season, remove any suckers as they'll take away nutrients from the plant, and you want to support the ripening of the fruit that remains.

When squash or cucumber plants have grown too large for the space they're in, it's okay to cut back a few leaves at their base with a sharp knife.

People who try to grow the largest pumpkin, watermelon, tomato, and so on, usually

Pinching

Pinching can be done throughout the growing season, but you want to be sure the plant is actively growing (which most houseplants won't be in winter, for instance). For plants that will need to be pinched more than once—annuals, herbs—start early in the season.

Deadhead

This one's easy. Remove dead flowers as soon as they've faded.

Disbud

Disbudding a flowering plant requires you to know the difference between a leaf bud and a flower bud. As soon as the buds are large enough that you can tell which is which and decide that they're big enough to keep growing, you can remove one or more flower buds to encourage the buds that are left to grow larger and showier. Unless you live in a frost-free climate, there's little purpose in disbudding in the fall.

Cutting Back

When a gardener cuts back a plant, the timing is almost always dependent on the reason for pruning. See the sections in this chapter on individual groups of plants for specific advice about when to cut back different kinds of plants.

Deadheading

Pinching back mums

prune their plants to reach their goal. They limit the number of secondary vines and also the number of fruits on those vines by cutting off the excess, leaving just one or two fruits that will naturally grow bigger without competition from other fruits.

The next chapter on decorative pruning will introduce another type of pruning with which you may not be familiar. Like grooming, it can make a big difference in the appearance in your plants, but in a delightfully creative and fun way.

CHAPTER 12

Decorative Pruning

U ntil now, we've talked about pruning as a science—if you make a specific cut at a definite time on a particular plant, the result will be what you expect because you've followed scientific principles. But now's the time to allow your creativity and inner artist to come to the fore. It's simple to make your yard distinctive with a couple of techniques. Topiary shrubs are evergreens that are sheared to a desired shape. This might be a boxwood shrub trimmed into the form of a dog. Or a yew cut into a series of round balls one above the other on the trunk. You're limited only by your imagination. Espalier (Ih-SPAL-yer, or ih-SPAL-yey) is an old technique of training a small tree or shrub against a wall to form an attractive pattern. Instead of pruning because you need to, you pull out your pruners and hedge shears to have fun and be artistic.

How to Create an Easy Topiary

The easiest type of topiary to create—and good for beginners—is called a standard. It usually grows in a large container and is kept on a porch, although there's no reason it can't be placed out in the yard, except in cold-winter climates. A topiary standard is a bare stem or stalk of a plant that's topped with a ball of greenery. Plants that make good standard topiaries include some vines: bougainvillea, creeping fig, creeping jenny, and English ivy. Mature rosemary is also excellent if you live in a climate where it's fully evergreen all year.

Place the plant in the container of soil and remove all stems except the one that will be the trunk. Then position a stake in the pot next to the trunk and attach the trunk to the stake with twine (green is good so it won't be noticeable) so it will stand up straight. Using a figure 8 to tie the two together will help ensure that the twine won't rub against the trunk and damage it.

Now, start pruning the plant. You'll want to gradually pinch off the side shoots from the trunk so that it stays free of stems or foliage. Once your trunk reaches the desired height, pinch out the terminal bud (see page 16). That will cause the shoots below to grow more vigorously, creating that round green ball you want.

As the foliage begins to grow at the top of the trunk, wait until each stem has 4 inches of new growth and then pinch all back by an inch or two to just above a new bud. This creates dense new growth.

As you go along, keep removing all stems that try to grow on the trunk. Also cut out any shoots that appear at the base of the plant, attempting to become a second trunk.

Once the standard has developed to your satisfaction, continue to remove all growth from the base of the plant and along the trunk. Shear or lateral prune (with hand pruners) the lollipop of foliage at the top to keep it bushy but neat. Do this during the growing season.

How to Create a Shrubbery Topiary

You've seen these living sculptures in pictures of elegant English gardens—and at Disney World. They're not difficult to create, but they do require plenty of patience since the original shape may take several years to develop fully; frequent pruning to keep it that way is essential from then on.

Start by choosing an evergreen shrub from our list (page 127) of good topiary shrubs, making sure you get one that's hardy and grows well in your area. (You can create topiaries from deciduous shrubs, too, but they'll be bare all winter.) It can be any size, depending on what sort of form or shape you plan to create. A camel or dinosaur obviously will call for a larger shrub than a cat.

About 6 months after you've planted the shrub in a spot where it will receive

Topiary shrubs are attractive and fun, but they do require regular trimming so they don't grow out of shape.

good sun on all sides, and it's growing well, begin pruning to create the shape you want. You will need to make some thinning cuts (page 20) to remove branches or stems that will interfere with the desired shape. Then lightly shear (page 19) or pinch off by hand or clippers the ends of the stems to create the shape you want. This also increases desirable growth on the outside of the shrub. As new growth appears, prune off wayward stems once to three times a year to maintain the shape. It's fine to shear needled evergreens or broadleaf evergreens that have small leaves once a year to maintain bushy growth.

Good Shrubs for Topiary

The best shrubs for topiary are those that are evergreen, grow slowly, and can be pruned repeatedly.

Alberta spruce

Arborvitae

Bay laurel (sweet bay)

Boxwood

Canadian hemlock

Japanese holly

Juniper

Leyland cypress

Monterey cypress

Myrtle

Pyracantha

Yew

How to Create an Espalier

Originally, espalier—training a shrub or tree against a building, wall, or support—was used to train fruit trees in ornamental two-dimensional patterns. George Washington espaliered fruit trees at Mount Vernon, which can still be seen today (and are very attractive). It's an old technique, originated by the Romans and making a comeback today.

Once you've decided on the spot where the espalier will go (the ideal is a wall or support that's 10 to 15 feet high and faces east or north so plants don't warm up too much), it's time to choose the plant you will train to the wall or support. Our list (page 131) includes the most commonly used plants for espalier, but the most popular by far, especially for home use, is pyracantha, or firethorn.

Our illustrations on the next pages show some of the designs or patterns that you may want to train your espalier to. But you can also find dozens more on the Internet if you'd like something different. You may even choose one because of the romantic names given the various geometrical

It takes quite a bit of pruning to maintain an espaliered fruit tree, but its attractive appearance is an asset in the garden. And it takes up less room than a traditionally pruned tree.

shapes. Choose a design before planting the tree or shrub you'll be espaliering, then use sturdy wire to trace the design on the support. Attach the wire so that it's about half a foot away from solid walls or buildings, allowing air to circulate freely. If possible, keep the horizontal wires 16 to 18 inches apart. Then plant the 3- to 4-foot-tall shrub or tree at the base of the pattern, near the center. (If you're growing more than one plant in the espalier, plant them 12 to 20 inches apart.)

You may start with a regular plant from the nursery or sometimes you're able to find one that's already growing on a small trellis, which gives you a head start.

Your espalier grows from a single stem or trunk, called a leader.

You direct and prune the new growth into horizontal arms (branches) that grow

Be fanciful with the shape you'd like your espalier to be. Draw it on paper first and then train it to that shape.

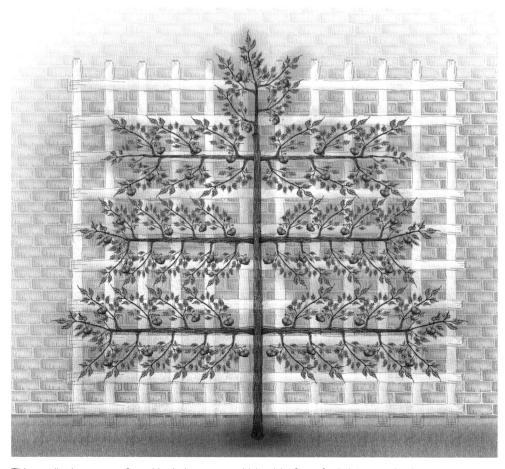

This espalier has a more formal look than some, which might fit perfectly into your landscape.

An espalier doesn't have to be large. This one was kept short and wide.

out from the leader, forming the pattern. Wait to prune until the plant has been in your yard for half a year and has produced new growth. The time to prune is in the winter or very early spring, except it's best to wait until after flowering to prune those plants that bloom in spring. Remove new growth coming from the soil at the bottom of the plant so you can maintain a single trunk. (In some patterns, the leader is headed back to about 18 inches or the height of the bottom wire. Then the stems that grow from it are trained horizontally. In other designs, the leader is allowed to grow straight up, with the branches that are allowed to grow off it trained to be branches or arms.) Tie horizontal stems to the support while they're young and flexible. Thin out those branches whose growth doesn't conform to the pattern and use lateral pruning (page 18) to cut back other branches to a bud that's headed in the direction you want the new growth to go. Continue doing this for about 3 or 4 years and your espalier should be established.

If you're espaliering a tree that generates edible fruit, take time to make sure you've left enough leaves to support that.

That doesn't mean the work is over, however. It's necessary to continue tying up new growth, direct and clip off wayward branches, and make sure the plant conforms to the pattern and doesn't overgrow the support. Yes, it's work. But for many gardeners, it's an enjoyable activity because it's creative

GOOD PLANTS TO ESPALIER

The best shrubs or trees for espaliering aren't subject to many pests, have long flexible stems, and produce either flowers, fruits, or berries. Fruit trees used for espalier should be dwarf ones that fruit on short spurs.

Apple tree

Cherry tree

Crab apple tree

Creeping cotoneaster

Flowering dogwood tree

Forsythia

Fuchsia (non-freezing climates only)

Japanese quince

Peach tree

Pear tree

Pyracantha

Witch hazel

and lets you interact with nature. And it sets you apart as doing something different. You may have the only espalier in your neighborhood, your part of the county, or even in your town.

Decorative pruning isn't for the impatient; it takes time and stick-to-it-ness. But it's one more element of the usefulness and beauty that can be produced when a homeowner picks up a pair of hand pruners or a small pruning saw.

USDA Plant Hardiness Zone Map

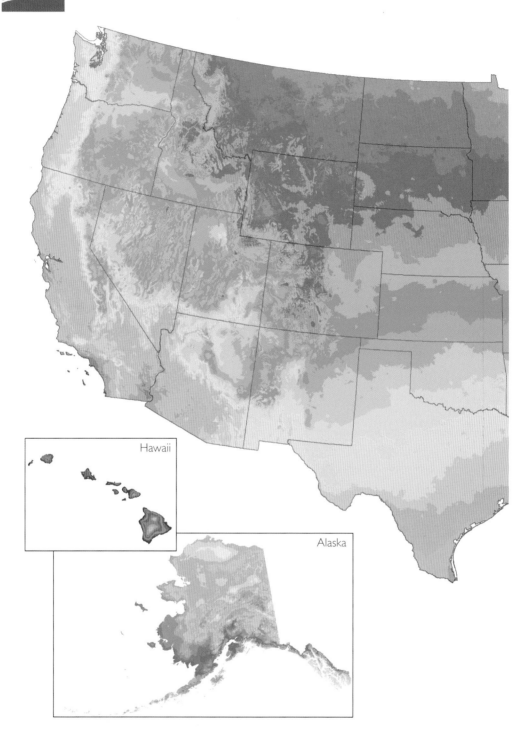

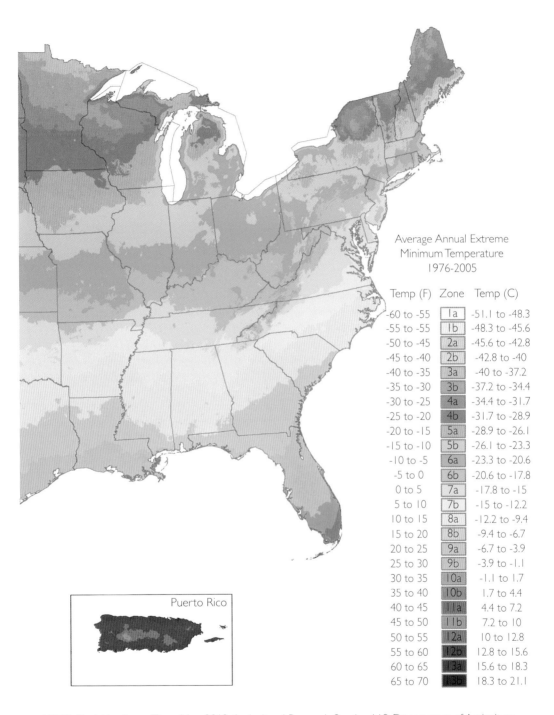

Average Annual Extreme
Minimum Temperature
1976-2005

Temp (F)	Zone	Temp (C)
-60 to -55	1a	-51.1 to -48.3
-55 to -55	1b	-48.3 to -45.6
-50 to -45	2a	-45.6 to -42.8
-45 to -40	2b	-42.8 to -40
-40 to -35	3a	-40 to -37.2
-35 to -30	3b	-37.2 to -34.4
-30 to -25	4a	-34.4 to -31.7
-25 to -20	4b	-31.7 to -28.9
-20 to -15	5a	-28.9 to -26.1
-15 to -10	5b	-26.1 to -23.3
-10 to -5	6a	-23.3 to -20.6
-5 to 0	6b	-20.6 to -17.8
0 to 5	7a	-17.8 to -15
5 to 10	7b	-15 to -12.2
10 to 15	8a	-12.2 to -9.4
15 to 20	8b	-9.4 to -6.7
20 to 25	9a	-6.7 to -3.9
25 to 30	9b	-3.9 to -1.1
30 to 35	10a	-1.1 to 1.7
35 to 40	10b	1.7 to 4.4
40 to 45	11a	4.4 to 7.2
45 to 50	11b	7.2 to 10
50 to 55	12a	10 to 12.8
55 to 60	12b	12.8 to 15.6
60 to 65	13a	15.6 to 18.3
65 to 70	13b	18.3 to 21.1

Puerto Rico

USDA Plant Hardiness Zone Map, 2012. Agricultural Research Service, U.S. Department of Agriculture.
Accessed from http://planthardiness.ars.usda.gov.

Index

Photo Credits

Dreamstime: pp. 68, 124

Tom Eltzroth: pp. 34 (right), 46, 84, 86, 88, 95

Katie Elzer-Peters: pp. 13 (top two, bottom left), 14 (left), 123 (top)

Endlesssummerblooms.com: pp. 35 (right)

Erica Glasener: pp. 35 (left)

Pam Harper: pp. 50

iStock: pp. 13 (bottom right), 14 (right), 26, 28, 30, 33 (bottom), 42, 54 (bottom), 56, 60, 77, 78, 82, 94 (top)

Jerry Pavia: pp. 27 (both), 51 (bottom)

Jupiter Images: pp. 40

Shutterstock: pp. 6, 10, 22, 34 (left and center), 51 (top), 52, 54 (top), 70, 90, 94 (bottom), 96, 119, 127

Neal Soderstrom: pp. 12, 41, 121, 123 (bottom)

Lynn Steiner: pp. 33 (top), 62

Meet Judy Lowe

Judy Lowe has had a lifelong fascination with gardening, starting as a child working alongside her mother, also an accomplished gardener. Later, Lowe began her garden writing career by serving as the garden editor at the Chattanooga Free Press and continued in that position after the paper became the Chattanooga Times–Free Press. Later she moved to Boston, Massachusetts, to become an editor at the Christian Science Monitor. Over the years, Lowe has shared her gardening wisdom and enthusiasm with countless numbers of readers.

She is a past president of the Garden Writers Association, a group consisting of nearly two thousand members of the garden writing community. Lowe's other credits and recognition include contributing articles to Women's Day and Southern Living magazines. She also appeared weekly in a gardening segment on television station WDEF-TV in Chattanooga, Tennessee.

Lowe's many awards include five Quill and Trowel Awards from the Garden Writers Association; a Special Communication Award for Tennessee Horticulture from the Tennessee Fruit and Vegetable Growers; the Exemplary Journalism for Home Gardening Communication Award from the National Garden Bureau, and many more. Lowe's proudest gardening moment occurred when a daylily was named after her.

In addition to this book for Cool Springs Press, Lowe is also the author of Tennessee & Kentucky Garden Guide, Herbs! Creative Herb Garden Themes and Projects, and Ortho's All About Pruning,

among other gardening books. She has lived in a number of different regions of the U.S., from the warmth of Tennessee to the chill of New England. In these areas she has experienced pruning all different kinds of plants from crape myrtle trees that grow very rapidly to lush, flowering rhododendron shrubs. She and her husband, Carlyle, who's known as the couple's official hole digger, currently divide their time between Tennessee and South Carolina. But no matter where Lowe lives, helping gardeners is one of her life goals.